MY LIFE PILE

A Compilation of Stories from the Lifetime of a Hunter/Gatherer

VIC BERG

Schiffer Publishing Ltd

4880 Lower Valley Road • Atglen, PA 19310

Library of Congress Control Number: 2013941948

Designed by Justin Watkinson
Type set in Engravers MT/Optima/NewBskvll BT

ISBN: 978-0-7643-4518-0
Printed in China

Published by Schiffer Publishing, Ltd.
4880 Lower Valley Road
Atglen, PA 19310
Phone: (610) 593-1777; Fax: (610) 593-2002
E-mail: Info@schifferbooks.com

For our complete selection of fine books on this and related subjects, please visit our website at www.schifferbooks.com. You may also write for a free catalog.

This book may be purchased from the publisher. Please try your bookstore first.

We are always looking for people to write books on new and related subjects. If you have an idea for a book, please contact us at proposals@schifferbooks.com

Schiffer Publishing's titles are available at special discounts for bulk purchases for sales promotions or premiums. Special editions, including personalized covers, corporate imprints, and excerpts can be created in large quantities for special needs. For more information, contact the publisher.

Front cover courtesy of Troy Cranford.
Back Cover courtesy of Ray Matthews.
All illustrations by E. M. Corsca.
Double-page Swan Sunset photo courtesy of Troy Cranford.

ACKNOWLEDGMENTS

The way that our community has come together and gotten
behind this set of stories is both heart-warming and humbling.
There are so many who truly want to see this project succeed
and who have so freely given of their resources to help us
toward that end. To all of you: Thank you!

A few of you, however, have gone above and beyond and need to be recognized:

Beth Storie is — how shall I phrase it? — a rock star editor who blessed me by asking if I'd let her edit "My Life Pile."

Let her? Let her! Holy crow! Black, black, no take back! How awesome is she? Ellen summed it up best when I pointed out a spot of prose that Beth had fixed: "Wow! She didn't do anything but make it sound more like you."

How do you categorize the confidence of sending a manuscript to your editor that you know to be very nearly flawless? Beth, thank you, thank you, thank you!

The person who gave me the best and most encouraging advice in the earliest stages of this project will be surprised to see her name here. **Faye**, I let you read the first drafts of the first stories while we were selling our wares at an art show in Whitestone, Virginia. What you said when you handed them back to me on Sunday fueled and encouraged me to continue.

"Vic, I don't hunt. I'm not against it, but I just don't do it, so I wasn't really expecting to like this as much as I did. You know, there were times when I was reading this, that if the show had ended and I had to give it back…I wouldn't have." Among other things, you told me not to be afraid of dialogue as I seemed to have a knack for it. If ever I got a pep talk from one of life's natural coaches, that was it. Thank you for caring.

Mom, you birthed me, you raised me, and you saw to my education. Sorry it took so long for me to get around to utilizing the latter. Thank you.

Vern, you raised me right. Thank you.

Vincent, my brother and tech-master, I don't know if we wouldn't have lost the entire project in cyber space several times were it not for your repeated rescue efforts and tutelage. It also helped immensely talking about our respective writing projects.

Ellen, my sweetie and companion for half my life, this was our project. You encouraged, typed, edited, consulted, and commiserated. When we married, I thought I'd found a teammate for this life…I was way right.

Everybody who has volunteered their connections in relation to sales and sales outlets, thank you, and thank you again. If we can distribute enough of these books, I'll get to write more. I'd like that a lot, thank you.

Pete Schiffer, you took a chance on a total unknown on the strength of a handful of pages of my life on paper. You have altered the course of my life with your support. Thank you.

And finally, **Bill Veasey and Shannon Dimmig** — wildlife artists extraordinaire — what can I say? You are responsible for my even beginning this project in the first place. Bill! What got into you? Every art show we were both showing at ended up with you telling me, "Write a book, write a book, write a book." I finally started one just to shut you up already! Thank you the most!

CONTENTS

"Whatever you are,
be a good one."

– Abraham Lincoln

Photo courtesy of Troy Cranford.

PROLOGUE

In this book, I am trying to lightheartedly share experiences gleaned while my wife, Ellen, and I lived and supported our family as a hunting guide/fishing guide/outfitter. But, my beliefs keep stepping in, somewhat eking into the lightheartedness at times, as do my strategies as a hunter/gatherer — a hunter/gatherer who must somehow survive in a world where hunting and gathering seems an ancient and barbaric, certainly outdated, notion. While this is not intended as a treatise on how to live our life, I would be thrilled if even a few readers could find enough clues herein that would help them adopt a more naturally balanced lifestyle. Shy of that, a chuckle or two will suffice.

February in a tropical locale; every Sunday of the year that it's seasonal, you will find us on a nearly deserted ocean beach with friends. The rest of the time we're artists. We are extremely fortunate in that, for some of the above, people pay us, so since Ellen and I have been together, neither of us has had to hold down a "real" job. I get why some are jealous.

Before you get too jealous, though, you might want to remind yourself that living this guide/outfitter life is not without its trials. I do not think that one person alone could pull it off, and a spouse or partner who is willing to work with you as a teammate is crucial. I think that most aren't prepared for the stresses of living with the uncertainties of such an "easy" life. You won't learn about many of those stresses until you're in the middle of it, but I can offer up some hints on what you may be looking at. No, on second thought, I probably can't, as each person's trials will be unique to the situations that arise in running your own particular small business.

In my opinion, you can't really live this life and work for somebody else. Your boss will have too many expectations, like being strict about your hours and wanting you to work overtime and not liking it when saltwater runs out of your nose when you lean forward due to the pounding that you just took in the double overhead shore break surf session that you enjoyed right before work. Then there will be that morning off so you can go shoot a few ducks just because a nasty Nor'easter is blowing in…yeah, that's probably not gonna sit too well. Especially when coupled with the three days next week for the opening of black powder deer season…yeah…no!

But let's just say that, despite the above reality check, you're still hell bent on trying out this "easy" life. So now you've gone and blown off your day job to become, say, an artist. Okay, this is what you just did: Instead of working regular hours for steady pay you will now work twice as many hours for maybe a tenth of the pay. You now have no retirement plan, and a lottery ticket a week probably won't make that issue go away. You have no health care and no hope for reasonable coverage because you can't afford any, and any health issue you may need help with won't be covered now because that condition will be considered preexisting. You have no paid vacations, no company car, no gas allowance, no secretary, no staff, and no stock options. If you're not actually working or turning something out you're not getting paid. Heck, you don't even get paid for making something until it gets sold…and the check clears. Unless your kids are motivated and plan on taking out loans, they may need to rethink their college plans. Come Christmas, you will need to balance what you can give with how badly you need to pay your rent, your light bill or all the rest of your bills. Unless you already have it you can probably forget about the new boat you've been thinking about…and the Harley. Have I depressed you yet? No? Really?! Well then, you seem adept enough at denial that you may stand a chance at living this life. You'll need to bulk up on your self-absorption if you expect any level of success from here on out. If what you need to do is going to get done, you need to see that it happens. Nobody gets hurt as bad as you if it doesn't get finished. If you don't focus on your own issues, other folks are going to hijack your time and use it for their own projects with very little benefit to you.

What you'll need the most of to become even a novice hunter/gatherer, however, will be faith. And not lip-service faith; you'll be in need of real faith, biblical style faith! The "If I sit in this tree on the edge of this field long enough, 120 pounds of food will walk by for me to harvest" type of faith. By the way, you confirm this faith by spending a few weeks' worth of days in that tree until you are proven right! Of course at this point most will just call you "lucky."

"Yeah, he really backed into that one. Probably hit it with his truck iffen' you asked me. I bet that's it — probably runned the dang thing over with his danged truck. Lucky bastard!" Of course, you won't get any credit because to do so implies that this lifestyle might just work.

I believe in this life plan. I believe that it does work, but I won't know for sure until my end of days. Until then, may I leave you with the hope that your gun never misfires and that your aim is always true. We wish everyone our best in their endeavors afield and the humility to see the humor in our follies. Happy hunting, and enjoy....

Photo courtesy of Troy Cranford.

YOU NEVER FORGET YOUR FIRST

11/23/1963: Thanks to my Dad's, the Reverend Vernon Edward Berg III, log books, I know this was the date I shot my first duck ever — on my first duck hunt! It was a cool evening hunt that lasted from four in the afternoon till sunset. We were gunning along the Ashley River outside of Charleston, South Carolina, on a falling tide with a south wind blowing a little better than ten miles an hour.

In the Remarks column for that day Vern wrote, "VICTOR SHOT HIS FIRST DUCK! A trio of mallards decoyed — I missed a pair after Victor shot his." What Vern didn't write was how the brush around the blind was too high for me to see over and that I had to climb atop our wooden shot shell/ utility box to shoot, or about the still-warm heft of a big fat South Carolina mallard drake, or about the brilliance of the light-refracted green of the mallard's head reflected in the eyes of a young boy who had just gotten his first dose of what it is to be a man…the evident pride of the most important man in my world. Holy Crow, but wasn't I "ruint!"

LIFE PILE

"Man, I've waited forever to do that." He is admiring my dog standing by my side with the man's first-ever mature bull pintail in her mouth.

"Perfectly decoying birds. Perfect shot. Perfect retrieve. Perfect day. Beautifully scenic spot. Definitely, one for the life pile."

"What's that?" I ask.

"What's what?"

"What do you mean, 'one for the life pile'?" I'll always remember his explanation.

Photo courtesy Vic Berg.

"You know. Usually when a guy starts hunting or fishing, he's a blood-thirsty savage. He's not happy unless he's got a huge heaping pile of fish or game. Over the years though, the blood lust wanes and you enter the next phase of hunting and gathering. Don't get me wrong, you still enjoy a healthy pile of game, but you're more interested in trophy stuff; a twelve-point buck, ten-pound speck, a one hundred-pound cobia, stuff like that." He takes the bird I hand him, and after admiring it for a few moments he continues.

"Then you get to a point where the physical pile doesn't really matter so much. Instead, you continue hunting or fishing for the unique moment — the billfish jumping under a rainbow on a misty morning; getting a one-shot double by waiting for two birds to cross before you fire or seeing your puppy retrieve her first duck." He ponders quietly for a few moments then continues. "Actually, a dog's first duck, while a prideful moment, is usually half accident and of poor form. The real event is that moment when the light snaps on in your dog's head. That instant (he snaps his fingers) when a dog gets it. When he or she all of a sudden realizes what all the training has been for. 'I'm a retriever! This is my job!' From that moment on, the two of you are a hunting team with a shared mission."

I have to allow that the man is right. I've seen it in every dog I've owned who went on to be a hunter. One moment you have a reluctant and head-strong half puppy/half dog galloping about in your rig, carrying decoys to shore and acting the idiot. Then an event transpires and your dog freezes for an instant, head half-cocked. Invariably, they'll look back at you half-amazed and right then, right there, you can see it. The switch is flipped in your dog's head, and in that instant they get it. Then they charge off with purpose and understanding, and in that moment you get yourself a gunning dog. When the man next speaks it startles me out of my reflection.

"Yeah, I can tell you've seen it too, and that's my point. A life pile isn't a pile of horns or mounts. It's a pile of memories. It's special moments, unique instances, gems of time and memory that stay with you forever." He turns the pintail over in his hands and points at the bird's leg.

"You know, out of that flock of thirty birds, I saw the sun sparkle off that band," he reflects, indicating the Federal bird band on the bird's leg, pausing a few beats with a faraway cast to his eyes, absorbing the scenery and the day.

"Definitely one for the life pile!"

HOW I CAME TO OWN THE MARSH

I am the son of Vernon Berg, a navy chaplain,
a Presbyterian minister. He was also a duck-hunting fool.

As I said, I shot my first duck — a drake mallard — from a boat hide along the edge of the Ashley River outside of Charleston, South Carolina. Being that my Dad was military, we moved around a lot. Every two or three years the family would uproot then resettle as per the orders from the Secretary of the Navy. Part of the resettling process was learning where to hunt near our new home. Any Navy base is on the water, and if you have water you've got ducks, somewhere. All we had to do was find ducks we could access. My Dad wasn't above using his status as a preacher to get at the fowl.

Dad learned to hunt amidst the marshes of the Great South Bay on Long Island, New York. As a result, in later years, he was always partial to shooting black ducks and scaup, staples of the Long Island sounds during winter. One would be well advised not to get between the preacher and a decoying black duck.

My brothers and sister didn't care much for duck hunting, but I was crazed for it. Consequently, from the age of eight, my Dad and I were fairly inseparable gunning buddies. Throughout our moves, I was blessed to explore myriads of marshes, little known backwaters and bays. In particular, I have memories of the areas around Charleston, South Carolina, northeastern North Carolina, southern Virginia, coastal New Jersey, Newport, Rhode Island, and Lake Erie layout shooting just above Chicago, Illinois. Since 1978, however, I've settled very comfortably into my life here in Northeastern, North Carolina, nestled amongst the Outer Banks.

A brief sidebar at this point will explain how I ended up owning the prettiest marsh in North Carolina.

As an offshoot of my Dad's love of duck hunting he also began collecting decoys before it became popular. Any family trip would include a visit to one or several crusty old carver's, gunner's or collector's houses. The family was usually required to wait in the car while my Dad talked and traded, but I could usually exercise my status as gunning buddy to get at least a peak at the decoys and decoy makers of a bygone era.

I was in the shops of, and spoke to the likes of, the Ward brothers who were from Crisfield, Maryland, Hurly Conklin, all the Jobes', T.J. Hooker, the Veasey clan, Erleen Snow, the Waterfields, the Brunets, Bill Mackey, Dr. Starr, and Bud Ward, to name just a few. Also, and just as importantly, I've held in my hands the carvings of all the great decoy masters from Mississippi and eastward, which includes the works of Crowell, Hudson, Lincoln, the Wards, Masons (too numerous to mention), Dudley, Cobb, Verity, Shourdes, Elliston, and Perdue. I've also fondled everything from scoter decoys created by unidentified regional masters from Monhegan Island, Maine, to hollow little gems from the Delaware River. The folksy Carolina clunkers, Susquehanna flats factory birds, pretty painted brilliantly preserved Mississippi blocks and ingeniously designed New England beauties have shaped my views of the classic decoy. In the sense of living gunning history, I've been truly blessed. The man who founded Outer Banks Waterfowl (OBW) did so around 1960. His name was Jimmy Curling, and he was a native Outer Banker. In the summers he was the mate for boat builder and captain, Bobby Sullivan. In the winter, Jimmy was the boss and Bobby the helper for duck guiding. On the second to last day of the 1977 season, Jimmy had a boating mishap and drowned as he was returning to the marsh to pick up the day's hunting charter and return them to shore.

As one of Jimmy's best gunning buddies, his family called my Dad right away. At the funeral my Dad learned that they were going to get rid of Jimmy's marsh in Oregon Inlet, called Herring Shoal Island. The marsh is located across from a small bay to the south of the Bodie Island lighthouse and Federal Refuge, and it is just a bit to the north of the expansive Pea Island National Wildlife Refuge. Jimmy's marsh covers an area of approximately eighty-five acres, and when you factor out all the creeks and ponds, it encompasses forty-four acres of actual marshland and five permanent duck blind locations. Of course, as owners you'd also be able to freelance hunt anywhere on the island that the wind and conditions rendered the most likely to hold ducks.

When my Dad returned home from the funeral (he was then stationed at Great Lakes, Illinois), he realized he had a very small window of opportunity. I remember him coming up to me and asking my opinion. He'd never had much money, but he did have one of the country's premier decoy collections. The pivotal question we had to answer was this: Would we rather look at the birds on the shelves in our house or pintail and widgeon in the clear blue skies over Herring Shoal Island?

My Dad made the call that night. A wealthy buddy had been after him to sell the collection for years. Dad simply told the collector this was his lone chance. If he could find a suitcase, fill it with cash, and make it to our house by the following evening, my Dad might be disposed to negotiate the sale of some decoys. Two days later we owned a most beautiful marsh!

When Vern took control of OBW, there wasn't much to work with. He did have the marsh, which was very good, but there was virtually no client base. Jimmy, for lack of a better term, was organizationally challenged. He had a logbook, which sounds good at first, but the only information in it was last names, the number of men gunning, and how much was owed. That was all the information Jimmy ever needed because all of Jimmy's clientele came out of his summer fishing charters. "Addresses?" Jimmy didn't need no stinkin' addresses! If they wanted to hunt, they'd best get in touch with Jimmy themselves — and of course they always had.

About this time, Vern was diagnosed with Non-Hodgkins Lymphoma, most likely a result of being Agent Oranged during his tour in Vietnam. Despite the interruption caused by an aggressive regimen of chemotherapy, Vern set out to run a guide service. The first year was pretty much a wash. Allied with two guides and a small list of backups, all pretty much starved that first year. During the previous summer's fishing season, all the old clients learned of Jimmy's demise and, due to Vern's non-native status, shifted their business to other captains from the fishing fleet. Business was good for them. Not so for Vern and company.

The following summer, Vernon discovered advertising. *Ducks Unlimited* magazine brought in, by far, the most clients. Numerous other periodicals and print media were also explored and utilized. Many hunts were "comped" to outdoor writers in a bid to bolster a now-burgeoning mailing list. By the 1980-81 gunning season (the year after I graduated college with a biology/philosophy double major...which two better degrees could a duck guide have?), Outer Banks Waterfowl, Inc. was a steam-rolling juggernaut.

No one had ever advertised nationally for water fowling on North Carolina's Outer Banks in conjunction with access to Currituck County immediately to our north. Vern did some wheeling and dealing, eventually consolidating several smaller guide services. The calls came in and the days of starving through duck seasons were in the past. The 1980-81 waterfowl season was also the best in terms of ducks harvested, a record that held for three decades!

There was little room for me in the guide rotation that first year out of school. Vern had himself and my best buddy from high school working our marsh daily. Besides, Vern had a more pressing need that year: The service needed a duck plucker. Nobody else would do it. I had moved back home and hadn't gotten a job yet....

"Hey everybody, meet the new duck plucker."

In the two and a half years since Vern took over OBW, Inc., he had gotten the business humming with twenty to thirty gunners per day, two men to a guide, and the guide sits with you all day — that's a max of forty-five men in the marshes per day! The scene in the hotel parking lot each pre-dawn was hilarious. Guides and hunters with their dogs and their cammo...everything; their trucks, trailers, and boats flooded into the lot then dispersed like a smoke grenade at an out-of-control rock concert. Caravans grouped up behind their guide and then headed out until, eventually, there was nothing left but a parking lot devoid of everything but the preacher, his dog and his truck, which seemed to be permanently attached to his trailer and duck boat. He'd sit around with another cup of coffee and talk to the night clerk long enough for any phone calls to come in that might report broken down outboards to reach him. Barring that, he'd slide out and find himself a spot to hunt a few hours with his devoted brown dog on the days that he wasn't guiding.

In my first year out of school, we reached the one thousand-duck threshold before the season was barely half over! Fowl, weather, and clients all cooperated. I couldn't start cleaning the fowl until the gunners returned each evening, so my work began well after dark. All birds gathered that evening needed to be cleaned, packaged, and returned to the hotel coolers prior to the time the hunters were checking out. That first year it seemed that I was pulling two to four all-nighters per week, cleaning ducks over the duration of the gunning season. The upside was twenty to thirty dollars per hour, cash. The downside was duck lice and being too tired to do much gunning myself. Even though I was the owner's son, believe me when I tell you, I started at the bottom and worked my way up.

The benefit of starting out as duck plucker, however, was that I was there to greet the gunners each evening. I got the stories of the day first, all the hits and the muffed shots — those rare situations that last a lifetime on the back shelves of a water fowler's mind. It was wonderful being totally immersed in ducking and goosing.

The other benefit of being the duck plucker was watching the gunning Reverend work his crowds. He needed to organize the next day's hunt the night prior, and the process started every evening at 7 o'clock. If he could, he met everybody in the hotel bar, where a little noise and confusion was expected and encouraged. All money due was collected prior to your first day's hunt. I learned that lesson early on! Things just work better if you get the money up-front.

The hunters who had gone out that day were showered and cleaned up by then, and those arriving that day were raring to go. There was an older two-man group over there and a twelve-man group from Michigan just showing up. On the other side of the bar was an eight-man group of police officers from Pittsburgh, Pennsylvania, talking to a group of seven podiatrists with only one vehicle between them. All told, it was a ginormous camper/hunt camp on wheels. On the other side of the coin, Vern had a list of all the guides, their limitations and the geographic areas each guide could work.

Everybody wanted to buy the Reverend a drink and hear a few duck stories. Pretty much, he delivered. Around 10:30 in the evening, everything is about lined up, as Vern shakes hands in greeting with the elderly two-man group. Told where they were going to hunt the next day and for what, you can see them stiffen noticeably.

"No, we're not going to hunt Currituck. We're here to hunt divers. That's all we want. Divers! Preferably cans."

Monkey wrenched, totally! Vern hustles off to rearrange most of the magic he has just spent the last three or so hours creating.

The saying in Oncology is that if a patient lives five years past diagnosis, they get to call him cured…good for morale in a brutal field of expertise, I guess. You're a survivor! Vern passed, six months beyond that date. It was in the spring, with a full load of memories fresh from the previous gunning season; the last duck taken on his last hunt was a drake pintail. Anybody who'd ever spent a day afield with Vern agreed that was only right. Violent electrical storms and tornados raged across the region the night Vern died. Those of us who knew him weren't surprised, because his was a huge soul to be ripped from the earthly plane. We kind of expected the weather to rage as a result. He spent only the last ten days in the hospital, and we all agreed that, too, was good.

I took over the guide service full time just prior to the 1985-86 water fowl season. For four years I ran the business full bore until one specific evening when I heard myself apologizing in advance. "Tomorrow's going to be slow, but I promise you'll get this (or that) the next day." I knew that his guide for the next day was to be a slacker (he, fortunately, owned one of the best blind locations in the county) who was afflicted with intermittently recurring substance abuse issues, and I could, honestly, only hope for the best in my client's regard as I was way over-booked. "Your guide the day after tomorrow is the hot guide with the hot blind...."

The client kind of flinched and gave me a bit of a look. At first I put it off on him as being, "one of those difficult hunters." The next day in the blind, during one of those slow times of the day, I started thinking: I have worse guides and filler guides; I have good guides with bad blinds and mediocre guides with good blinds but bad equipment. Hmm.

Soon thereafter I embarked in the direction of guide servicing that we use today. I kept the best and weeded out the rest. One decent-sized group and we may be booked for the day. The people appreciate it or they don't return. We shoot lots more fowl and have lots more fun, and on no occasion do I look in the mirror and see a North Carolina pirate looking back, nor do I ever feel the need to apologize in advance.

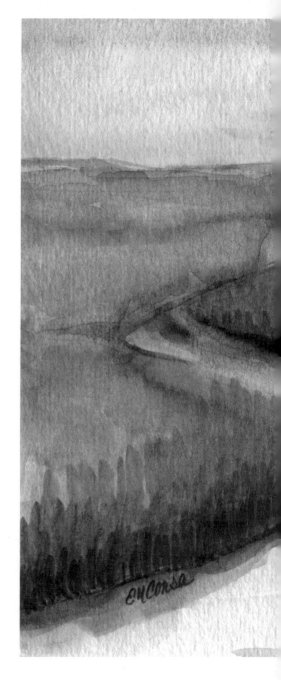

Photo courtesy Chris Price.

#130711_Wo De Sheng Huo_Int_F1_A.b...

DUDE

"So, other than shooting ducks,
this marsh ain't worth nothing, is it?"
"What?" The question caught me off guard. "I wouldn't say it that
way, but now that you have, I'll have to agree. This marsh most
certainly isn't worth nothing. Exactly that, as a matter of fact!"

"That's what I thought," Dude continues on, double negatives and all. "You say you can't build anything on the marsh because it's a protected environment. Cause of the saltwater, you can't grow crops." Dude shoots me a side-long glance. I surmise a kind of a "he's just too lazy to plant crops in a saltwater environment" kind of look. That nothing suitable grows there naturally is immaterial.

On cue, he continues. "I'll bet there's some crop that'll grow out here. You should figure a way to grow crops to feed the ducks." Without missing a beat, Dude keeps the narrative rolling negatively along. If one wanted to define what a "Nattering nabob of negativity" was, this guy could serve as the poster dude. "When are we going to get more shots? If you'd figure a way to grow crops on the marsh, we wouldn't have to wait like this."

"Dude's just about got under my final layer of skin," I muse to myself in the quiet of my thoughts. "Must not rise to bait!" I urge myself. I bit back the snappy retort and instead occupied myself with focusing on the area of sky above and to either side of the Bodie Island lighthouse. Early afternoons, like this is, that air space is where I expect our next opportunity at a shot to appear.

My communication skills are kind of hampered by the fact that I can't recollect Dude's name. Went right in one ear and out the other this freezing predawn when I shook his hand and introduced myself to him in the 7-11 convenience store parking lot.

"Shoot," I think to myself. "Anybody who knows guides knows that their brains are full in the morning. People can die if we screw up." A guide thinks of little else until the boat is launched and we're safely to our hunting blind. Then, every one of the 107 decoys in the boat have to be placed and anchored precisely to my liking — no help from anybody. I'd just have to touch everything they might do to try to help. Nothing personal. I'll probably take help picking them up this evening, but setting decoys in predawn's dark, things have to be done exactly right. Otherwise, when the day dawns, you find the tides and the wind are working against one another and things aren't right. Birds won't "pitch" and you're not so much hunting as you are just sitting out in the cold — and I don't like just sitting out in the cold!

"Dude's, a better name for him anyway," I continue in the privacy of my brain. "Dude is a dude — a shooter and a body piler-upper! Certainly, he's not a sportsman. No student of nuance, this one. He's been doing this negative stream-of-consciousness thing since before daybreak. Jeez. Is this what being a duck slut feels like?" Quiet reflection doesn't seem to be working so well for me.

"Wild celery grass." I say it all of a sudden then not anything else.

Takes Dude by surprise, just the three words. He's flummoxed by the silence after. Before he can rev up again, I continue.

"A thousand acres of it, created by a just and loving God and put in front of us right up to the shoreline. Best natural food for wild water fowl in the world on the right day. When the water drops out, ducks swarm to it and gorge themselves. Today's not that day, though. Sorry about that." I continue quickly to try and keep Dude from returning to the negative.

"Today, because of the west in the wind, the water's high. When the water's high, the marshes flood, especially around the refuge's ponds. When the refuges flood, seeds, bugs, and other stuff are floated up." I warm to my subject but know better than to let the lecture lag.

"A bird's like any other critter. He's going to feed where he can get the most nutrients for the least amount of effort. Throw in not getting shot in the face, and that's why gunning's slow today. Oh, that and it's a clear and sunny fall day on the eve of a hugely full, harvest moon. You just need to relax. We're already doing better than we have any right to expect on a monumentally 'blue bird' day like this is." I can't help but getting in a little dig as I keep on with my edification.

"If it was me and my murderous bastard buddies hunting here today, we'd have six or seven good birds in the box already. That hen pintail and gadwall you've managed to rag out will feed you and your family another day. So, like I said, relax. We'll get some more shots, or at least we've got a way better chance here than we would back at the hotel.

"By the way," I add, a cold look entering my eyes. "I've had a chance to think about it and what you said earlier about the marsh being worth nothing is...."

Thankfully (because what I was just about to say was probably going to have a seriously negative impact on my tip that evening), at that moment, I spied five widgeon over the lighthouse, five hundred yards out and three hundred yards up, wings already cupped and coming right at us from the refuge. Past beautiful and straight to spectacular was that pitch by that flock of widgeon.

I'd like to say that at that moment fowl began to flood to us. And we shoot limits. And Dude, of a second, gets it.

"It" being that it's not the pile of death and feathers that matter but the celebration of life that we get to experience en route to another fine meal of healthy wild game provided by ourselves, our patience, our skills, and the benevolent forces of nature...but I don't get to say that.

He whiffs on the five widgeon and another pair of drake pintail just before sunset as well. For me, though, it's but another beautiful day at Pintail Point.

Turns out that Dude's family won't eat any wild game. He's too...whatever... to cook it himself. So, at the end of the day, I get his birds, the thirty fat oysters that I picked up when I went for a wander at mid-day to escape the nattering for a while, and the cash paid for guiding...and a moderate tip.

Absolutely. This marsh most certainly ain't worth nothin'.

DOLLY WOULD

Gosh. This was back in the early '80s when Chris and his dog, Dolly, worked for us.

I'd been seeing this diminutive little bird behind one of our blinds for a couple weeks. I did a little research and ciphered out that the bird was a sedge wren. This bird is rare by wren standards, so it's very scarce in general.

I suggested to Chris that if he ever had gunning clients who were also birders, he ought to point the bird out to them. Any birder I've ever met is always thrilled to add another rare sighting to his or her life list.

Not a week goes by and Chris is picking up his check on Sunday.

"You know that bird you were telling me about?" Chris asked innocently.

"Sure," I reply.

"Well, my clients on Friday were birders and sure enough, neither had the sedge wren on his life list. In fact, one of the guys had been stuck on 999 birds for nearly a year, so he was real eager to hit the one thousandth-bird milestone. Anyway," Chris continued, "no sooner were we done with my mentioning the sedge wren when out popped the little fellow. Sat on a branch in that dead bush right behind the blind and 'chip chipped' at us as if to say 'hi!'"

Photo courtesy Troy Cranford.

28

"Well, that's awesome," I reply. "That guy must have been thrilled to nail down bird number 1,000. Did the bird give you a good enough look at it so that he could count it? Those guys can be real persnickety when it comes to a confirmed bird sighting."

"Oh yeah," Chris replied. "We confirmed it all right. Got him a picture with the bird as a matter of fact," he continued.

"What?" I ask, sensing more to the story.

"Yeah. No sooner had the bird hopped onto the branch and 'chipped' at us than Dolly got up, walked over to the bush, and glomped the bird right into her mouth."

"Oh my God," I gasped. "You mean Dolly ate the bird right in front of the guy? He must have had a stroke!"

"No, no," Chris soothed, laughing all the while. He had to stop and catch his breath before he continued. "No, she glomped the bird. She didn't bite it. She just held it in her mouth. You know how soft-mouthed she is." Chris is roaring now. "You could even see the little fellow's head poking out from under Dolly's lip as he kept 'chipping' at us."

"But the bird was okay?" I ask in amazement.

"Better than fine! She brought it to me and put it right in my hand. We got a picture of the two of them together! Then he hopped off into the bushes." Chris had to wipe tears of laughter from his eyes. "Believe me, the sighting was confirmed."

Chris is still kind of chuckling to himself. "You know, Vic, twenty years from now, when the guy thinks about this trip, he's going to forget all about the ducks, and all he's going to remember is that silly sedge wren." He paused just a beat then muttered under his breath almost to himself as he stuffed his check into his back pocket. "Did I tell you the guy tipped Dolly?" he asked. "Gave me a fifty buck tip, then gave me another twenty bucks and made me promise to buy something nice for the dog. I'm headed to the store to buy Dolly a steak right now. Gotta go," he said as he turned to leave.

Then he affirmed what any guide already knows,
"You've just got to love this job."

MERGANSER JERKY

I believe and participate in hunting/gathering as integral to our lifestyle. I find it to be healthy and honest. There's a code that goes along with your hunter/gatherership — a code of Do's and Don'ts that is not to be trifled with! *Don't* overharvest. *Do* identify and target specific energy sources at specific times of the year. *Do* harvest your game as humanely and efficiently as is possible. *Don't* be a dick.
(I toss that one in, but it's a good rule, nonetheless.)

Photo courtesy Troy Cranford.

Sow what you need for the year during the season in which it is the healthiest and most harvestable. Process and put up what you have taken and then move on to the next energy source. Try not to fall in love with any single endeavor. If you inadvertently harvest more than you can use, barter the rest. The boat ramps that I put in and out of also service the offshore fleet. I'll trade a pair of good ducks for a yellow fin tuna at the docks whenever I can in the evening. We are both thrilled to score the variety at the end of a day afield. Just apply that to everything.

Oh, yeah, also never miss an opportunity to help out your harvest species. An example is to bring back an oyster's shells after you've consumed the inhabitants. Sprinkle the empty shells back where you originally picked them up. Oyster babies need something solid to attach to in order to survive and grow. In only three years these baby oysters will be mature enough for you to eat. Do that every opportunity and you'll always have oysters. Bada-bing! Apply this practice to everything else, too.

Now factor in the myriad of energy sources. Throughout the span of a year, we attempt to harvest the following: wild turkeys, blitzing blue fish, flounders, blue fin tuna, yellow fin tuna, red drum, black drum, cobia, clams, sheepshead, some sharks, trigger fish, stripers (both ocean and sound), my limit of five deer, many ducks, oysters, geese, doves, rabbits, and an occasional squirrel. And mahi! You can't forget the mahi-mahi.

So, to get more specific, never wipe out your prey. Respect your prey. Learn their habits and mannerisms so that, at time of harvest, you can do so as humanely and efficiently as possible.

You owe it to the critters and to their ancestors to have sharp knives, a sharpener and the skills to not waste anything. Learn to sharpen your stuff. Learn anatomy and how to skin and field dress. I know it's gruesome. (The gruesome factor weeds out a bunch of would-be hunters/gatherers.) Get over it and learn to clean game the right way while wasting as little as possible. As I like to say, it's only fair to the critters.

Take what you need when most easily available, then move on to your next quarry/endeavor. Always allow enough survivors so that your quarry can regenerate. You survive as your prey survives. Help take care of them. Barter your excess whenever possible. Between our artwork and guiding for hunting and fishing, we can usually trade for our wants; needs, however, usually require cash.

If you are clever you can hunt cash the same way you hunt critters. Identify your prey. Find bait that attracts it and its best season for harvesting. Present your bait, cull what comes to you and when you get enough, move on. No gloating. It's not respectful and reduces both you and your prey. Respect is shown by properly cleaning and storing your harvest, whatever it is. Rejoice with friends and share your harvest. Then move on to the next resources available.

Enough of that for now. Let's change the subject. Beliefs and rules can be tedious. Compared with tedium, I prefer irony. Believing and living your beliefs can get interesting.

This, in the absence of a smoother segue, brings us to mergansers. Mergansers present conscientious water fowlers with a dilemma. On the one hand, they're great targets. They fly like ducks. They set their wings and land into the wind like ducks. They're naïve, and very often they fly when other ducks won't, even on blue bird days. On the other hand, they don't taste good.

No, not just not good. They taste bad. Really, really bad! The merganser's meat is very blood-infused, which leaves the taste strong and gamey. The taste is further affected due to diet. Their food source is fin-propelled, so when cooked, merganser presents to your palette in an offensively fishy manner.

Add fishy to strong and gamey in general, and one can imagine how bad the flavor must be.

Nothing you can imagine does justice to one's first taste of roasted merganser. When made into jerky, think of what a fish's liver must taste like, then add in a texture of damp sawdust (except sawdust is easier to get out of your mouth and throat). What's a gunner to do?

"Mergansers fly like ducks."

"They taste bad."

"They set their wings and glide into your decoys like ducks."

"They taste bad."

"Mergansers are legal game."

"They taste bad."

"Mergansers are really good targets."

"They taste bad."

"You can shoot a lot of them."

"They still taste bad."

"They don't even count against your duck limit!"

"I'm sorry, but we both know any merganser you shoot is not getting eaten."

"A drake hoodie is pretty enough for mounting, but I probably won't."

"They taste bad!!"

"I've got a brand new shotgun and I really want to shoot something."

"They taste really, really bad."

(Are you catching on to the dilemma? Unless you have a use for a critter it should not be harvested. Period! Otherwise, you're behaving like a "kill-monkey" [a murderous bastard] who need be punished in wrathful ways by powers beyond our understanding.)

"What?"

You'll curse yourself. If you kill something and then dishonor it by not caring for it properly, you'll hex yourself. You'll probably have to endure a week's worth of skunk days to atone. Or your outboard will swallow a dose of bad gas. Or, you'll lose your boat plug or your high dollar sunglasses overboard. It's just not worth messing with for the thrill of killing something that you have no use for. Never throw away game! If you're gonna' kill it, you're sure as heck going to clean it and eat it. At least that's how my Daddy and all my other mentors raised me.

Having said all that, the early and mid-1990s was horrible for water fowling along the mid-Atlantic Coast — really slow gunning with pretty, warm weather. There just weren't that many birds to be had...except for mergansers. They were everywhere. Flocks of twenty to thirty of the danged things! Decoying from high up, just like pintails would!

So here you sit. A duck guide. You're out in the wild from before sunrise to after sunset in a blind the size of a packing crate. You're with a couple of young South Carolina bucks with a case of shotgun shells between them and brand new Christmas shotguns.

The sun rises to reveal a cloudless sky devoid of wind. Not only have you not popped a cap all morning, but also the only ducks you've seen have been a pair of blacks a mile off an hour or so ago.

But the mergansers are everywhere. Every time a boat moves anywhere on the sound another flock or two gets up and wings their way into our decoys. The boys are past restless and there's still a lot of light left in the day.

I know it's wrong, but I'm desperate. We're looking at a long day ahead of us, and I can tell all these guys really want to do is to pull the trigger. I know I'm probably going to Hell for it, but I've no choice but to throw the mergansers under the proverbial bus. So, after this inner battle over ethics comes to a point, the conversation continues.

"We need to start shooting the mergies." Both guys' heads spin to survey me.

"But, don't they taste bad?"

Obviously, they've been raised right. They don't want to shoot what won't be used. But they really want to shoot, badly, and a lot.

I know my tip's at stake, but I'm a crafty guy. I explain that mergansers can be eaten: just cut them up in little pieces and cook with a lot of other stuff and in a thick sauce. It also helps to be really hungry. They remain unconvinced; however, I can tell that they're open to persuasion. It's time to play my ace.

"Then shoot 'em for me," I innocently suggest. "I clean 'em and feed 'em to my cats. They love 'em. I either buy cat food or feed 'em the merganser. Either way, money's money, they'll get used." Long story short . . .

The next flock pays dearly. "Feed 'em to my cats" works every time. But, there's the rub: I don't have any cats. I am stuck with my ethics, however, and the mergansers!

For better than a couple of weeks, I'm bringing home up to fifteen mergansers a day, but I'm too scared of cursing myself not to clean the fishy rascals each night. Eventually, I have a couple sacks full of merganser meat. What in the heck am I going to do with two sacks full of merganser breasts?! I've got to use the meat or I'm cursed, sure as all get out.

Then the light bulb goes on over my head. Inspiration! I know what I'll do. Jerky. Merganser jerky. Just spice the heck out of it and hide the merganser flavor. Brilliant! What could go wrong?

So, I have Ellen whip up a super-spicy marinade, cut the merganser breasts into thin strips and let 'em soak in the marinade for three whole days. I throw the strips into the dehydrator and hope for the best.

They're finally done. It's Sunday afternoon, my day off. The Redskins are playing. I'm kicked back and don't have to meet tomorrow's gunners until this evening. Let's try a taste of that jerky.

I take a strip and pop it into my mouth. Mmm…not bad. Spicy! No taste resembling a fish's liver. Mmm. I chew a bit more and my saliva infuses the dried, spiced merganser. Not bad…Mmm.

As is the case in most mariners' mishaps, things go awry in a blink of the eye. At precisely the twenty-third second after the jerky enters my mouth, everything falls apart. Literally! The meat dissolves into a powdery paste. It coats the mouth's interior. And then it hits you.

Magnified at least a thousand times as I remember it, a rankness heretofore unparalleled. Think a fish's liver allowed to putrefy for days in a Tupperware® container left in the hot sun. Now open the container and inhale deeply.

"OH…MY…GAWD!"

It's in my mouth! The first wave of concentrated dried merganser flavor about makes me retch. I do retch…around four of my fingers as I try to claw the now saliva-damp merganser puree out of my mouth.

OH…MY…GAWD…MAKE IT STOP!

It takes gargling, swishing and spitting to finally get the taste out, a whole beer's worth, a lot of spitting and even more swishing. "My God, but that's putrid," I gag to myself.

It tastes so good at first. I survey the big pile of jerky that remains. "Maybe that's just a bad piece from the bottom of the pile or something. Hmm. I've put a lot of effort into this jerky. It is said that a sure sign of insanity (other than being a water fowler) is to repeatedly perform the same act while expecting different results. I try another piece.

I'm lulled into a false security by how good and spicy the marinade is. Mmm-mmm. My saliva moistens the dried meat. Awesome marinade…mmm. At precisely the twenty-third second of being in my mouth, the wheels fall off the apple cart again. Meat to paste, again, just prior to the wave of nausea personified that is the flavor that I've assaulted myself with…again.

"OH…MY…GAWD!... AWWWWGH! My fingers are up to my third knuckles trying to claw the vile slime from my mouth. Waste another beer swishing, gargling, and spitting. Swishing and spitting. Swishing! Spitting! Swishing!

Just then, my twelve-year-old stepson walks in.

"What 'cha doing?" Stephan asks.

I swear the boy can smell jerky from ten miles away. Upwind! He loves the stuff. I've seen him eat a venison shoulder's worth in one sitting. Usually when I make a batch of jerky I give him his whole share up-front. Then I try to hide the rest. Like that's ever worked out for me.

"I jerked up all that merganser that's been in the fridge," I answer.

"There's a lot of it!" he says eying the pile of jerky. I'm sure he's trying to gauge how big his windfall is going to be.

"Yeah, but it's horrible."

"Really?"

"No. I mean it. I'm still on the verge of yacking."

"Really!"

Oh? Now, it's a challenge. This ought to be interesting. "Yeah," I answer, "it starts out pretty good, but when it goes bad it's really bad. And quick...you go from bliss to puke in the blink of an eye."

"Really? What are you going to do with it all?" Now he's really intrigued.

"I guess I've got to throw it away," I answer.

"But what about cursing yourself?"

"Yeah. I've been thinking about that, but there's nothing for it. When the taste goes bad, it's really, really bad."

"I hear that," is his reply. "Let me try a piece," he says as he chomps onto a big chunk of jerky. "Mmm. Nice marinade. Spicy! Mmm-mmm. I don't know what you're talking about." He chews blissfully, imagining that he's about to score the whole jerky batch for himself. "This is good."

"Wait for it," I caution. "Any second now...."

"I don't know what you're talking about," he reiterates. "This is goo...OH...MY...GAWD...GAWWWWH!" He's three knuckles deep in his mouth trying vainly to scrape it clean. "GAWWWWH."

I'm just about weeping I'm laughing so hard. "That's what I'm talking about!" I bellow, as Steph goes about wasting half of a two-liter bottle of ginger ale gargling, swishing, and spitting. Swishing and more swishing. Many times more! He's a fun-loving kid and he's laughing too...between the swishing and spitting.

Finally, as things calm down, Stephan looks up at me with his big cornflower blue eyes.

"That's awful," his voice a sigh. "What are you going to do with all this jerky?" he laments.

"I guess I have to toss it. I hate to, but I don't feel too guilty. We tried to eat the 'gansers. Jerkying 'em's just a bad idea. Man, when they go bad, they go ALL THE WAY BAD. You're chewing along and right about the twenty-third second...BAM. That wave of flavor just sucks so badly."

Steph eyes the pile of jerky wistfully.

"There's just so much to waste..." his voice trails off... but suddenly he brightens. "Let me try another piece," he says it excitedly as he pops another merganser slice into his mouth. He chews blissfully while keeping an eye on his watch. "Fifteen, sixteen, seventeen, eighteen," he intones and then–gulp–he swallows the whole bite. He waits. Tense. As if he's waiting for a bomb to go off. Arms spread. Knees bent. A couple tens of seconds go by. Suddenly, he brightens. A huge smile is on his face. He snags another slice and, while following the second hand of his watch, swallows the whole bite at the twenty-second mark.

"Can I have it?" he asks gleefully. The whole jerky pile? "Hot dag!"

Twice bit! I'm done with it. "Sure. Take the whole pile. I did my duty. Have at it," I say with a grand sweep of my arm. "It's all yours."

So, all is well in my neighborhood. We settle down to watch football, Steph munching contentedly away on the merganser jerky while keeping a vigilant eye on the second-hand of his watch.

"Sixteen, seventeen, eighteen, nineteen" gulp. "Are you sure you don't want some?" he offers sincerely. "Just swallow it at twenty seconds and it's fine."

I demur. I'm not putting anything that can be that nasty back in my mouth.

The first half of the game is over and Steph has consumed, like, half of the pile of jerky. He's got a smugly contented look on his angelic face, when all of a sudden I can literally hear his stomach rumble from across the room. I watch as he looks down at his belly and then assumes his watchful stance — arms spread, feet splayed. Another belly rumble as he looks up at me bug-eyed.

Then, "BUUUUURRRRRPP," out it comes. Quiet at first, it built to a prideful crescendo. It's at the second P of "BUUURRRRPPP" that Stephan's face goes green.

OH…MY…GAWD! GAAAAAWWWWW!

I swear I see his knees buckle a bit and a tear in his eye as the now one hundred-percent concentrated flavor escapes his mouth at the end of the burp. I wet myself laughing. Funnier still is that with all the air he swallows at the twenty-second marks, he rips merganser burps on occasion all throughout the second half of the Redskins game. Each time followed by:

"BUUURRRPP. OH…MY…GAWD…GAAWWWW!

HOW TO MAKE YOUR OWN
Merganser Jerky

Basically, when I make a marinade for wild game, it mostly consists of any hot sauces I have in the door of my fridge. The following is just a guideline.

INGREDIENTS:
Six duck breasts or
one deer shoulder sliced very thin

For marinade, mix together
in freezer bag the following:
   1/2 cup Worcestershire sauce
   1/2 cup cider or balsamic vinegar
   1/4 cup olive oil
   1/2 cup pickapeppa sauce
      or other hot sauce
   1 cup A-1 sauce
   1 tablespoon red pepper flakes
   4 garlic cloves, minced

Marinate for 1-2 days and then arrange on trays of a dehydrator and cook until the meat is brittle. (Usually overnight.)

TIP: *Spray the bottom of the dehydrator and trays with PAM and they will be much easier to clean.*

KEEGAN'S REDHEADS

By the end of the week, Currituck is close to froze up and the blinds in the inlet get a crack at their teal. Justin comes to the inlet on Saturday to escape the ice up north. He's rewarded with, on top of a fun day gunning, a crack at a flock of fifty or so teal — an awesome sight. I watch this drama unfold from my blind, 700 yards away.

One guy is peeing behind the blind, one guy is off to the side of the blind with no gun, Justin is lying in the weeds outside of the blind keeping a watchful eye with both eyes closed and his gun ten feet away. Now add in a flock of fifty teal tumbling into their decoys, wings locked and tertial feathers crackling audibly from the strain of their free fall from 150 yards up. Woo-hoo! They were lucky to get the three teal they did get. What a sight though!

Talking about sights: Keegan will have to get the award for the most awesome experience of the season. No, not the lost in the fog part…Okay, admittedly, he's a little late getting tied out. He's told the guys he's guiding for that it's already legal shooting time and to load up and take anything (not near him) that comes across the decoys while he tends to some chores in his boat in the boat-hide. In a snap, they're loaded up and looking into the eerie gloom of first light.

As Keegan tells it, it seems like he looks down to do something for about a second, and when he looks back up it almost feels as though the wind is somehow being pushed out of his chest. Just as he looks up, he's faced with a gargantuan flock of redheads swooping into his spread — from 300 yards up! No, really gargantuan! There's close to 3,000 to 5,000 birds. Bud and I see the flock from two or three miles away. We estimate the flock to be three-quarters of a mile long and a bit under a half-mile thick…and they're dropping right into their faces!

When he tells me the story — and I've heard it more than once — he ends up ultimately dissatisfied in not being able to accurately convey the magnitude of the moment. The pure awesomeness! "No, Vic, you can't understand. I look up and that whole flock is pushing down. Pushing down from three, four hundred yards up! Pushing the air down in front of it! You can feel it." The sound (he makes a whooshing sound). Then another, more heartfelt whooshing sound! Another, stronger still. Then he just has to look at you. He realizes words cannot describe the experience.

"So, they came all the way in?" I ask. "Close enough to shoot?"

"Oh, yeah!" He gets the faraway look and tries again with the whooshing sound. "If any of us had thought to pick up our guns…."

THE FINE LINE BETWEEN TWO AND TEN

What I say about the fine line between ten and two never rings truer.

Photo courtesy Vic Berg.

I have a hunt with a couple of guys from South Carolina on the season's second to last day. I've just gotten the decoys placed where I want them and have put my now empty boat (I rigged every one of the 114 decoys that spend the season in my flat-bottom gunning bateau) around to its hiding spot for the day. If we don't get any ducks today, it won't be due to a lack of decoys.

I watch the blind from the cove, some 700 yards distant, where I short-tie my anchor line and hook my boat to the marsh's edge. I'm aware that the decoys came out of the boat a little slowly this morning being that I had to unwrap a single decoy's line and toss that decoy, then grab the boat, then unwrap another decoy and throw that one and then grab the boat.... That's the pace for the entire decoy spread. A quick check of my cell phone tells me two things: All my other guides (seven of them) must be where they're supposed to be and with whom they're supposed to be with; and two, my guys need to be paying attention, it's shooting time.

I glance back at the blind just in time to see six widgeon appear out of the gloom and coast across their decoys. I see an arm attached to a pointing finger waving above the brushiness that is the Pintail Point blind. In my brain, I'm screaming, "Shoot...shoot dang it, shoot!" It's been a long, tough season and the last thing I want to see are some Audubon-acting fellers pointing out decoying fowl with their fingers.

"Sweet honey mustard!" I shout in my brain, "Point with your guns! That's why we brought 'em!"

After an entire season of unusually high water and west winds, we're finally standing in the teeth of a proper Nor'easter: twenty to twenty-five knot winds with gusts to forty...thirty-five to thirty-eight degrees...spitting sleet and snow... low clouds...water levels fallen radically to ankle-deep levels that coastal Carolina gunners covet. Perfect weather!

I'm still mumbling under my breath about the six widgeon as another widgeon pair appears out of the darkness, right over their decoys. Bam! Ba-Bam! Three shots, muffled by the near-gale force winds, rumble across my marsh. Both birds fall. I'm happier. Two birds in the box! I finish hiding the boat and head toward the blind.

All of a sudden, two more birds appear, wings set over the decoys. Bam. Ba-bam. Bam. Those two crumple and fall. Oh, yea! I'm way more happier. The guys scramble out of the blind and head after the downed fowl.

By the time I'm halfway to Pintail Point, the guys are diving back into the blind and are grabbing for their guns as two more widgeon are sailing through the decoys. Ba-bam. It sounds like one shot, but both birds fall in unison.

I get to the blind and we already have one full, six-bird limit. Every one of the birds is a nice, fat, beautifully plumed drake widgeon.

Another pair flies around the corner to our left and promptly sets their wings.

"Sucked right into the hole," as the saying goes. It takes all three of us, but there are no survivors.

Finally we get our comeuppance. We all three totally whiff on a coasting flock of four widgeon. They are peeping and whistling as they fly in and nine shots later are peeping and whistling as they fly out, headed for the safety of the refuge a thousand yards upwind. Honest, they aren't twenty-five yards out and right at eye level. We just totally whiff.

In the next twenty minutes we make short work of two singles that can't resist the lure of 114 hand-painted, properly placed E. Allen decoys in front of the phenomenal marsh point upon which sits the legendary Pintail Point blind. It's almost too much fun…too much fun that you can't get enough of.

It is now 8:15 in the morning and already we're sitting on ten widgeon, eight of which are beautiful drakes. Other than the first flock of six that they didn't shoot at, and the flock of four that we whiff on, these murderous rascals have knocked down ten fowl out of ten! It almost makes a guide want to tip his clients.

Of course, this gets me giddy with confidence, so lo and behold, what do I do? I voice the thought that firmly places a curse on our blind for the rest of the morning.

"Ten birds in the blind by 8:15. Let's see if we can beat the record that Justin set for this blind this season and be limited with eighteen birds by 9:10 or earlier."

Of course, when you check in on us later that morning at 11:30, we haven't had another shot. Me and the stupid hole in my face that doesn't know how to shut up!

Anyway, my guys decide it was a beautiful morning. With ten birds to take home, they're only a few off their limit, so what-the-hey, they'll call it a day. I'm going to quit also with thoughts of a late season "coma nap" in mind. Then I make the mistake of glancing back at the blind as we head off toward the fishing center just as two regal black ducks sail through the decoys that I left set out. I alter my plans. After all, it is the second to last day of a tough season. The weather is hideously perfect and I'm going to pretty much nap the entire month of February anyway. I'm dropping these guys and their birds off at the dock and I'm coming back out to fun hunt this evening.

Remember how my guys make the best of the fowl they have to shoot at in the morning. Well, not so much for me in the evening.

There was that pair of blacks when we were in the boat. Then I miss a pair of redheads with three shots. I follow up a half-hour later by watching three widgeon zig when they should have zagged on their fourth and final trip across the outside edges of my decoy spread that I never pull the trigger on.

Oh yeah. Then there was the lone drake pintail I only took a farewell shot at. He drops in over my right shoulder from behind me and from across the marsh. They almost never come from there.

Of course, that gets me watching that spot, so I don't see the flock of perfectly pitching cans that swoop in from my left until they're exiting the decoy spread to my right. And finally, for the coup de grace, ten minutes prior to sunset I spy three birds falling into my spread from around the corner to my left. Their wings are locked up and they seem to be headed straight to the open spot in the middle of my decoy spread, which is right in front of me. One hundred yards, seventy, fifty, their wings tilt. Fifty-five yards, sixty…What?

Gadwalls, dang it, you short pitching so and so's. I shoot all three shells, counting the last one, which is a three and a half inch BB. Of course my first shot is at about sixty-five yards, and nothing falls…right away. Finally at the far edge of my bay, at about 650 yards from where I'm standing, a bird finally falls out. A fine line between two and ten indeed. I manage to prove both sides of the theory on the same day.

I often remark to folks about the fine line between two and ten. Pay attention and see what is coming to you, while not flaring stuff off. Point out fowl within shooting range with your gun instead of your finger. Know where your safety is without having to physically look, and hit what comes to you. Ten birds or better can be available on most days. Don't do these things and two birds will more likely be the case. Either way, the only difference in the two scenarios is the total if your attitude remains the same.

Photo courtesy Chris Price.

JUSTIN SCHOOLS ME

Another thing that sticks out for this season is the number of federal leg bands taken. Yeah, you heard right, duck "bling." Counting the band I find on a floating, dead pelican, we account for eleven federal bands this year. Two of the three banded brant taken sporting jewelry have one on each leg. Besides the five found on brant, and the floating pelican, we also harvest two pintail and two redhead drakes that were federally banded. We round out our band harvest with a big, old, red-legged, male black duck.

If I am remembering right, I believe the national average for fowl per bands is about 400:1. We beat those odds by a bunch this year. Water fowlers love their "bling." One of the only reasons I lock my truck during winter is because of my call lanyard with five attachments for calls on which I've also affixed my lifetime's worth of federal bird bands. When not in use I keep them stored, hanging from my rearview mirror. This gives the calls time to dry out from the hot air coming from my defroster, which I leave running wide open when I'm driving to or from the inlet — the better to dry my various gloves as well, which got wet during the day, on the dashboard. Between my calls and bands the mojo that hangs on that lanyard would measure through the roof.

How's this for a day's total bag?

BEST DAY SOUTH OF OREGON INLET: 1/22/10

Six redheads, their limit of three drake pintail, six widgeon (one of which is a drake Eurasian widgeon), a greater blue bill, two big male American black scoters, and four brant. To top the day off, they're limited by noon, and one of the brant has a band on each leg.

BEST DAY IN OREGON INLET: 1/11/10

I've been (what I call) sumo ice wrestling for the past week. When the temperatures get frigid enough and the sound starts to freeze, sheets and/or chunks of ice are propelled by the tides through your decoy spread throughout the day. If allowed to flow through your spread, the ice will eventually drag off your whole rig. The only way to forestall this is to physically wrestle (steer) the ice around before it can snag the decoy's lines and drag them off. Where I hunt it is shallow enough to wade, so the battle that is waged with the ice all day is even more personal.

I hear persistent rumors of large flocks of bluebills eating up my Colington diver blind. Justin is totally frozen out in Currituck. In my infinite wisdom, I decide to let Justin gun Pintail Point and I head to Colington to avoid another day of sumo ice wrestling. This just goes to prove that even with all the experience in the world, it's still possible to over-think any scenario. It turns out that, over night, the temperatures fall even lower than in days past. The next morning I end up breaking ice the entire four miles to my diver blind. Once there, I find the sound frozen from my shoreline to a point three miles out. And broad sheets of ice are shifting. All morning! No sooner do I get a couple dozen decoys out and get back to the blind then another sheet of ice is starting to drag another cluster of decoys. Then, you've got to go rescue those decoys, and by the time you get back from doing that, there's another cluster getting all hooked onto another ice sheet, and on and on, till you finally decide to quit and give up on the day.

Meanwhile, about an hour after shooting time, I get a call from Justin. It seems that it has frozen just enough that the ice in the inlet is more solid, and it has locked in and is no longer shifting at all. To top it off, Justin informs me that he has a natural open water pocket exactly in front of Pintail Point. You guessed it. I get one shot at a hen canvasback from my blind all morning and wrestle massive sheets of moving ice the entire time. At certain points we are, justifiably, concerned that the ice might drag the entire blind under, boat hide and all. The chatter and groans of the ice breaking up against the blind as it is driven past by the tide is beyond unsettling. There are times that the flowing ice shakes the blind so badly that I am on the verge of abandoning ship.

Justin, meanwhile, limits out by 9 a.m. His total? There are thirteen widgeon, their limit of three drake pintail, and two greater blue-bills arranged neatly along the gunwale of Justin's boat in the picture he sends me via my phone. I think to myself that he's enjoying this way too much. I am happy for the young guys who Justin guided that day, though. They got a life pile hunt for sure.

Currituck handles high water much better than Oregon Inlet does. Therefore, they pretty much rule up to the point when they get frozen out around the second week of January.

How's about this day's total in Currituck?

12/21/09: Eight teal, three black ducks, two drake mallards, a drake pintail, a drake gadwall, and two brant! To make a great day better, one of the brant has a band on each leg!

Photo courtesy Troy Cranford.

SOME GEOGRAPHY, SOME HISTORY

My Dad first hunted ducks along the northern Outer Banks of North Carolina in 1960. He started bringing me along with him a couple of years after that. The Banks are a remote area even now as they aren't on the way to anywhere. If you want to get there, you need to make a special trip no matter where you begin. Back in the early '60s the Banks were downright desolate. From where the "hard road" started south of the Virginia border, along the whole length of the Banks to the free ferry in Hatteras Village — a distance of about 120 miles — there were only three stoplights to impede your flow on the roads in those days.

In the town of South Nags Head, just to the north of Oregon Inlet, the National Park Service had (and has maintained to this day) twenty duck blinds located just off the ribbon of highway that runs upon the ribbon of sand that connects the town of Nags Head to the northern end of Hatteras Island.

Before I get involved with talking about the Park Service duck blinds, though, I think it would be good to give a brief (I'll try, really) description of the area's topography.

In truth, North Carolina's northern Outer Banks are an enormous estuary system made up of a glorified 200-(and some)-miles-long sand spit that is separated from the mainland, its entire hooked length, by huge brackish-watered sounds. The Banks themselves are no more than two miles wide soundside to seaside, and at some points are only a couple hundred yards wide. As you'd expect, large ocean storms can and do wreak havoc on a fairly regular basis. The most recent was in 2011, when several new inlets formed during Hurricane Irene. We on the extreme northern Banks got our butts handed to us, but Hatteras Island was devastated.

Technically the Banks are a series of really long, really narrow sand islands, as there are inlets scattered every thirty to fifty miles along its length. As mentioned earlier, the northern Banks begin a few miles from the Virginia border, where Back Bay enlarges to form the Currituck Sound.

The Currituck Sound narrows about thirty miles to the south near the town of Corolla on the seaside and Currituck on the mainland. This narrowed area is shallow, brackish, and full of naturally-growing submerged grasses that ducks covet and is fairly riddled with marshes and marshy islands that are fabulous ambush points for gunning wild water fowl. Hugely famous with water fowlers, this Currituck Sound area has a rich tradition with generations of watermen having plied her shallow bays.

Where the marsh islands begin to fade away, the water opens up again and forms the northern end of the Albemarle Sound. While the lack of marsh around the Albemarle offered few areas to hunt from, clever gunners countered this by inventing devastatingly effective gunning platforms called sink boxes. The term "hunting platforms" would be a misnomer since a sink box, when seen on dry land, would look to be a one-person coffin with a gently arched deck from its upper edge that flows out and down to where the water would meet it.

When put into the water, the contraption would float and could be moved and anchored where needed. With the addition of the weight of the gunner and numerous heavy cast-iron decoys placed on the arced deck, the coffin would sink to a point where the gunner lying in the box would actually be out of sight below the water's surface.

Carefully anchor this low-profiled structure in the midst of several hundred hand-carved duck, goose, and swan decoys far from land and in the open sound with a freaking metric ton of cracked corn under the entire rig, and you can easily understand why the U.S. Government decided that they were just too danged effective and banned them entirely around 1920. Baiting for waterfowl was also banned around the same time, although there are those who have, evidently, not heard this news.

The southern edge of the Albemarle Sound occurs fifteen miles south of Currituck and is demarked by another choke point where the mainland juts to the east in the town of Point Harbor. The town of Kitty Hawk lies to the east on the oceanfront. A one-lane, wooden bridge to the Outer Banks was first completed across this two-mile-wide span in 1932. South of this choke point, another twenty miles, you find Roanoke Island (Ground Zero for the successful white/Anglo invasion and conquest of North America; I'm not proud of it, but a fact's a fact), where another series of spans and causeways has been maintained for better than a half-decade. At this point the comparatively huge Pamlico Sound opens up and continues to the south another hundred miles to the towns of Cedar and Harker's Island near Morehead City.

This brings me back to the Park Service blinds in South Nags Head — these blinds are in a beautiful marsh that was deeded to the U.S. Government when the Off Island Gun Club consolidated its membership in the 1940s. Their deed to the Government states that the United States National Park Service could have the land, but in exchange, the Park Service had to provide free duck hunting to the public throughout every entire duck season thereafter. If the public is ever deprived of their right to hunt the land, it is to immediately revert back to its original heirs. I'll try to spare you from too many details, but it'll help to know how the blinds work as well.

The U.S. Park Service takes applications to gun its Bodie Island marsh no sooner than September 1st every year. Each person (on the whole planet, actually, excluding felons) is potentially allowed a maximum of six days that they can reserve the right to hunt one of the twenty blinds. There is no limit to the number of days you can hunt on a walk-up basis. If more than twenty people apply for the same date, the Park Service holds a drawing and selects the twenty people who get blinds that particular day. Each person chosen can bring one other person to gun with him. The blind is yours for the entire day or until you limit out, quit, or leave the blind.

If fewer than twenty people get reservations on any given day, the rest of the blinds are given out on a first-come, first-served basis. On most any day there are a few blinds left over for the overflow crowd due to the practice of gunning buddies applying for the same dates. If they're both drawn to hunt on the same day, each one draws his own blind and then decide which of the two blinds should work best with the predicted weather and wind for that day. They hunt that one and turn the other blind back in. The other blind is then offered to the overflow hunters.

I got a little ahead of myself. Once you've been selected to hunt a particular day, you need to show up the morning of your hunt at 4:30 to sign in. At exactly 5 a.m., each of the twenty lucky hunters takes their turn and draws a circular brass wafer from a brass tube. The brass wafers were mixed up prior to being put into the brass tube. Each brass wafer has a number from one to twenty on it. That number corresponds to one of the twenty blinds. The blinds are numbered from the north to the south along Highway 12. The northernmost blind is number one and the southernmost is number twenty. Vern's favorite blind was always number six, and he'd be fairly shameless in his attempts to work a trade in order to get it. If, once everybody present had a blind and there were any undrawn blinds left over, you could return your wafer and try again till you got what you thought was the best blind remaining.

At the end of each hunt, you have to return to the Ranger Station to record your kill for the day on a sheet of paper that is always left in an unlocked covered box that anyone can access. At the end of any hunt, it's nearly impossible to not want to read everyone else's kill sheet to see how your hunt compared.

To make an already too long a story a little shorter, over a period of a few years, Vern kept seeing Jimmy Curling's name atop most day's totals. On the days that Jimmy's name wasn't at the top of the list, he was usually second only to Vern. Being that both usually gunned alone and both hunted Chessies, it wasn't long before the two had introduced themselves and teamed up and hunted the best blind drawn between them. This was a bad day for ducks everywhere. As it turns out, it was a very good day for me, however.

Once they hunted together a bit, they soon realized that Jimmy's male Chessy (a 145-pound behemoth and retrieving prodigy named Smokey) and Vern's female Chessy, Abby, hunted splendidly together. The dogs actually got to a point where they'd take turns retrieving downed fowl. Vern and Jimmy got along as well.

Almost immediately after they started gunning together, Jimmy, whose family owned a motor court named the Buccaneer Motel, gave Vern his own cottage to use for every season thereafter, until Jimmy's untimely drowning on the second to last day of the 1977 waterfowl season.

Even though Vern was obligated to his military career and we moved around the country every two or three years, the draw of the northern Outer Banks was inexorable. Every gunning season where it was possible, Vern would take me out of school for a week to gun with him and his cronies in North Carolina.

In a nutshell, the above history illustrates the geography that served as a backdrop for me to build the man that I have vied to become during this lifetime. Duck hunting, and its unwritten laws, can be a metaphor for the hunting/gathering life plan. Vern talking to Jimmy because each were successful water fowlers, mostly due to their adherence to steadfastly doing things right, while they looked over the kill sheets after a day's hunt in the Bodie Island Marshes, led to me writing this line forty-eight years later. Who knew? Who knows? You put your best effort into everything you do just because it's the right thing to do, with no idea of what, or how, things might work out.

Everything comes to those who do what is right for no other reason than it's the best option. Look at it this way: Nobody ever got the break of a lifetime in reward for putting in the minimum amount of effort necessary to be able to call a job done. You never know what mote of extra effort will be the mote that gets you noticed and causes your dreams to blossom.

Compare it to setting out your decoys in the morning. If you just roar up to your blind in the dark of morning and begin flinging out decoys with no regard to weather conditions or organization, you're probably going to have less than optimal results.

But you don't do that. You look into the wind and feel it on both of your ears at the same time so you know exactly where it is coming from. You visualize the flight path that flying fowl could traverse that would best benefit your success, and you strive to make that happen. Very often, success while water fowling may come down to moving one specific decoy out of a spread of a hundred five feet in one direction or another.

"How do I make them do that?" you ask yourself...and then you spend the rest of your life trying to answer that question. Do it right and you shoot lots of fowl; do it not right and you very often find yourself just sitting outside in the cold... as mentioned earlier, I do not like just sitting outside in the cold!

A CAMEL'S STRAW

I'm hunting on my own, which, as a full-time guide
and the guy who owns an awesome marsh
and everybody knows it, I don't get to do very often.

As I remember the day, it is early afternoon, edging
toward the end of another gunning season. The sky is as
clear and as blue as Carolina can make it. I haven't seen
a bird in hours, but that hardly matters. This is just a fine
place to be on a cold winter's day.

I've just been awakened from a mid-afternoon late season
brain-fade by the sound of distant snow geese. Arranged to
the downwind as I am, I can see that nothing is imminent
without moving my head. Slowly, I scan the rest of the 360
degrees. Still don't see anything.

Photo courtesy Troy Cranford

The unmistakable barking of more snows! I shade my eyes to check around the sun. Nothing. No, wait…What's that?…Holy sweet honey mustard…Looky there. I've never seen birds so high in the sky. They're just barely visible as black-trimmed, white, sound-producing pin pricks in the clear blue of the sky. If, as I remember reading somewhere, space is only twenty-some miles up, then these guys must be better than twenty miles up there. The word "squadrons" comes to mind. Wave after wave passes straight overhead but just below the realm of space. I marvel as the multitude passes, the sounds of a distant cacophony resonate now.

Finally the stratosphere-scraping flock is almost past. I figure to myself, what the hey? I've got 120 silhouette snow goose decoys spread about behind my Pintail Point blind. They're arranged in small groups of three to five members each to better resemble a collection of family groups feeding together.

I give a few tentative voice yelps, a few nasal barks, and a "ner'ronk" or two for good measure. As expected, the hoard moves inexorably on. I throw a near perfect "ner'ronk" the flocks' way for good measure and…What? No?! Yes, way!

The last bird of the entire 10,000-member flock suddenly peels out of formation. No way!

Then three more peel off. Then five behind them, then twenty, then fifty, and then 150 are peeling out of formation.

"Holy crow in indigo!"

Now, 500 peel off, with 2,500 behind them and another 4,500 wheeling behind that crowd.

"Hot dang. Hot dang. Hot dang!"

The whole freaking 10,000-bird flock is in a mind-befuddling, slow-motion, smoke-in-reverse spiral straight over my head! I'm looking up at an enormous snow goose tornado!

The top of the spiral is big and loose and open, but the lower the spiral descends the tighter it gets.

Minutes go by, at least ten, maybe fifteen. As the flock finally nears my marsh, they spread out. An aerial blanket of 10,000 barking, yelping, ner'ronking greater black-winged white geese are all trying to land at once!

It's going to take the entirety of the 180-acre marsh that I am on the tip of to land them all. They're all — every one of them — milling around ten to twenty feet up. All of a sudden it seems that the flock realizes that my 180 acres isn't going to be enough to hold them all. The flock, as one, begins to lose interest. They're beginning to rise again. The sound and confusion of 10,000 swirling winged bodies virtually sucks the very oxygen out of the air.

Suddenly, I snap out of my awe stupor and grab my old Belgium Browning auto five.

Lately, the gun's been operating as a one- or two-shot automatic…just shooting back-up and cripple finishing as is usually my job, it's not been an issue, but…I hope for the best as I rise up above the rim of my blind, gun already to shoulder.

Blam!

The first one's so close that I have to shoot its wing for fear of ruining the meat. From the corner of my eye I see the wing fly off on an odd trajectory. Macabre! I may need therapy later, but right now I'm too focused on my next shot to think about it too hard.

Blam!

On my second shot I've held up long enough to let two birds align in space. Both fall out dead, one crashing the side of the blind on its short descent.

In my mind, a third shot. Blam! In reality, nothing! I squeeze the trigger again.

More nothing. I'm incredulous!

For my third shot, I had four fowl bunched up in a space the size of a small truck tire and in my sights at twenty yards.

As I squeeze the trigger in vain yet again, I focus closer and notice the second shell's husk poking halfway out of the gun's ejector. By the time I can clear the second shell, all that I'm left with for targets is mayhem and white butts flying away. I lower the old automatic and watch as, this time, the white smoke that is the escaping flock spirals up properly.

I proudly survey my three greater snows as I quickly dispatch the first with my last shell, now chambered. A triple is a triple after all, but it's hard to let go of what could have been. Man! On that last shot alone I could have had at least four birds…DANG!

It's not long afterwards that I retire my old Browning auto-fives. I've had me an epiphany! You just never know. Every now and then, maybe only a few times in one's lifetime, things go insanely and incredibly right.

For that moment I now carry a pump gun. As long as you don't feed it rusted-out shells, it shoots three times, every time with low brass number eight shot to three-and-a-half-inch BBs. Really, man!

Those four geese occupied the space that a microwave oven would take up. Click!

Last straw, man, last straw!

GOOSE CALLING

Photo courtesy Troy Cranford.

Jimmy Curling was by far the best goose caller I ever met. He never used a man-made call of any type. He was a voice caller.

Don't get me wrong. I've been privileged to hear some of the best goose music ever performed by humankind. I got limits hunting with multiple world champ Glenn Covey and have sat awe-struck listening to Erleen Snow at decoy shows, but no one ever talked goose like Jimmy talked goose.

A proper call has two segments: the low guttural first sound is immediately followed by the higher, resonating second note. It has to be similar to a whip's crack. Jimmy often told me it was kind of a mix between country music and Tyrol yodel to achieve the transition between the two notes. That transition is the key to a proper goose call. (A Tarzan yell also contains those transitions, but not as sharply or as forcefully defined as in a goose call.)

It was Mr. Curling's opinion that if a kid didn't learn to call geese before his voice changed, he'd never be able to execute a proper call. To prove a point, he asked my Dad to do a bit of calling for us. Now as a bit of background, my Dad, Vern, and Jimmy, were tight as gunning partners. Vern had witnessed Jimmy's prowess calling geese on many occasions and was so enamored with the effectiveness of voice calling that he had practiced endlessly (it seemed, to my chagrin) to perfect his own voice call.

Just the week before, as a matter of fact, my Dad had managed to call a trio of fat Canada geese into his decoys. Vern was plenty full of himself. When Jimmy asked him to demonstrate, he nearly dove at the chance to perform for his mentor. "NAR-ONK, RONK, NAAARO-NK, AHH-RONK."

Bless his heart, but he simply sounded awful. He finished off with his strongest effort yet. "AHHHRO-NK, RONK!" Jimmy let this performance settle in for a full minute. It seemed that it took that long for our ears to unclench. Kind of like the effect of biting down with your teeth fillings onto a ball of aluminum foil while somebody else fingernail-scrapes a blackboard.

"Now see, son. Your voice has finally all but changed. If you don't practice, and I mean this week, that's the most you'll ever be able to hope for." We all laughed. Vern didn't take it personally. He had called in that bunch of geese the week before, after all. Besides, Vern knew that if I learned now, I could do his calling for the rest of our days together. I learned that week.

Even though I was only a kid (twelve), my Dad would take me out of school for a week every year that he could to go gunning with him and his hunting buddies. It wasn't our fault that school inconveniently coincided with duck season. Could life be any better for a kid? We were nearing the end of the week and I had been "ner-onking" my head off at every chance. In my mind, I had perfected a right passable goose call.

Hunting in a dense fog in the public blinds of the Bodie Island marshes, I'd managed to turn a lost gander back toward us. The goose and I conversed for a full minute as he zeroed in on my calling. You can't imagine a child's disappointment any more than was mine when a gun erupted from the next blind over. Even though I never even saw that bird through the fog, I knew for a fact he was coming to me. That other SOB shot my bird! I had been inconsolable as I'd never shot a goose of my own before.

We were in one of Jimmy's blinds in Kitty Hawk Bay the next day. It was late morning when a gaggle of about thirty Canadas came winging into view from the north.

"Now's your chance," Jimmy urged. "Make up for yesterday."

I honked once or twice, timidly. A couple more honks and I was warming to the endeavor. I tried a few more honks and then a yodeling barrage that sounded like a flock and a half of geese all by myself. In twenty seconds, I'd near about "ner-onked" myself sick. The birds never veered. Not even a bit. I felt an elbow dig into my ribcage.

"If you're going to change the minds of geese, you got to talk to the boss," Jimmy whispered.

"Nnng-onk."

"That's her," Jimmy noted. He matched her tone and inflection to a T with a honk of his own.

"Nnng-onk," she replied. Jimmy answered back. She called twice. Jimmy aped her note for note. The flock that had long ago passed us suddenly wheeled. At once, the rest of the flock went silent.

"It's you and me now, sweetheart," Jimmy gushed in a whisper. "Tell me what you want to hear." She replied. Jimmy answered. Back and forth it went. Note for note, syllable for syllable.

I thought we were going to lose them once when Jimmy's voice half cracked through the exertion, but he managed to add a few mewlings that reassured the boss goose and they again wheeled into the wind and, finally, into our decoys.

I got my first-ever goose that day. In fact, I'm not sure I didn't get the one my Dad claimed as well. Jimmy, he got the boss goose. He had to, he told me, because now it knew his voice.

Photo courtesy Troy Cranford.

PEA ISLAND DECOY SPREAD

Here's an innovative decoy spread I developed that works particularly well on a day when you're hunting and there are light and variable winds. I've dubbed it the Pea Island Spread.

I've noticed many times while observing birds at rest on the area's waterfowl preserves that a certain pattern occurs when mixed flocks of waterfowl are most at ease while feeding in shallow water.

First, the swan spread out at least twenty to thirty yards between each bird and virtually all are head down feeding. Around each swan, in a tight cluster, will be four to six widgeon that are thieving food from the longer-necked swans. On occasion there will be a tight cluster of different fowl, perhaps teal, pintail or gadwall.

The result is a loosy-goosy spread with a lot of empty spaces around tight clusters. Mimic this pattern and you'll be well-positioned, no matter which way the wind swings. There are always open landing areas for the birds to settle into.

It also helps if you shorten your decoy lines in these conditions so as to reduce tangling as your decoys change directions with the variable winds.

TOP DOG

Top dog position shifts around from guide to guide throughout the week depending mostly on which gunning party possesses the most skill, patience, and good, old-fashioned duck-luck. Thursday and Friday of this week provides a good example. Justin and Graham guide those two days. On Thursday, their two groups can tell the day is "blue birdy" and opt to bail around noon and head for that so-called family-friendly restaurant, Hooters, for libations and of course some of their famous wings. On that day Justin's group knocks down three blacks and Graham gets skunked.

Friday dawns as a mirror image of the previous day. Their two parties on this day opt to hunt till the very end of legal shooting time. Around noon, Friday's groups have about the same level of success as Thursday's. When Friday's parties hit the docks at dark that evening, however, the similarity of the two days ends. Justin's bag for the day is composed of two swans, two Canada geese, two mallards, a black, three drake redheads, and, unfortunately, two mature drake pintails that they knocked down but cannot retrieve. Graham's bag: two swan, four mallards, three black ducks, two gadwall, and four ruddies.

I'm always asked, "Are we going to shoot any birds this afternoon?"

I always answer, "I can't tell you till after, but the only advice I can give you prior is that you have a way better chance of shooting ducks here than you have of shooting ducks from Hooters. The only way you can have good luck is by keeping yourself in a position to be lucky."

As I recall, Woody Allen once opined that eighty percent of success is showing up. To that I'll add that the other twenty percent is sticking around.

Grilled Goose Breasts
WITH RASPBERRY MUSTARD SAUCE

If you serve oysters as an appetizer and then finish with the following recipe for dinner with twice baked potatoes and a salad, you will have a feast for yourselves! Should you have leftovers (not likely!), the meat makes a great sandwich also. We like our game medium rare, but if you prefer it cooked more, that's fine. A word to the wise, however: Wild game contains almost zero fat, so if you overcook it, it gets dry, strong, and tough. We recommend that you cook and serve wild game rarer than you might domestic meats.

INGREDIENTS:
One goose breast
1/2 cup dry red wine or balsamic vinegar
1/4 cup olive oil
1/4 cup soy sauce
1/2 teaspoon pepper
4 cloves garlic, minced

- Mix last five ingredients in glass bowl or freezer bag
- Add goose breasts and marinate 2-3 hours turning to coat a few times
- Grill on grey coals or medium-high heat of a gas grill about 10 minutes on each side, or till done to your preference. Let rest for five minutes. Slice thinly across the grain (as you would a London broil). Top with raspberry sauce.

Sauce
1 tablespoon water
1/2 cup raspberry jam (seedless)
1/4 cup Dijon mustard
1/8 cup lime juice (usually one lime)
1 tablespoon Worcestershire sauce
1 tablespoon coarse ground black pepper
2-4 minced cloves of garlic
1/2 teaspoon caraway seeds
1/2 teaspoon thyme leaves

Add all ingredients into a small sauce pan and blend thoroughly. Heat over low heat, stirring occasionally, for about a half-hour until the sauce is uniform.

THE TIP

The G.R.I.T.S. (Girls Really Into Shooting) go gunning with our guide Les. Photo courtesy of the Outer Banks Waterfowl.

Nearly everyone who hunts ducks does so for the thrill involved, the lightning quick reflexes, and sinew of man in flawless conjunction with a finely constructed shootin' iron.

"Take 'em…" Blam! Blam!...two Federally leg-banded, drake canvasback, floating belly up on the water…that sort of thing. What isn't emphasized in the many annals of hunting lore is that there is a lot of empty space between electrifying events.

Many, many hours have been and will be spent looking at empty skies, sometimes days on end boxcar, one after the other, between memorable shoots. The avid fowler knows and accepts this as unfortunate fact. In order to get to the good days, you're going to have to make acquaintance with many slow days as well. Eventually, what's left to do during slow days is conversation.

Nothing eats up big chunks of a slow-moving day like good conversation. A guide knows this. His tips depend on it, and as such, a good guide becomes a matador of gab. Avoid topics as emotional as politics or religion, but realize that, after the last blush of dawn, you're likely looking at hours of close interaction ere you head for the docks that evening hence.

This is one of the main reasons that water fowling enjoys the popularity that it does. Within the blind you can move around. You can talk. You can have snacks. You get to fire off your guns with good purpose every now and again. You drink coffee. Swap stories. Share stuff. Blow on noise makers (which is what duck and goose calls can be if in the hands of an overeager neophyte). It's not like deer hunting where you feel like your day is ruined if you so much as break wind.

Heck. When you're duck hunting you're encouraged to break wind. What the heck, when you're wearing chest high waders, you're just saving it for yourself later.

As a guide you never know what you may hear next, but the art is to keep the conversation flowingly copacetic-like so as not to get too spirited, but you want it to flow nonetheless. In this regard, then, it can be said that a good guide sets the tone in the blind and/or in the boat. Don't get people riled up when they're locked and loaded, I always say. Plus, as a guide is always aware, the tip's involved.

As such, I strive to maintain a good, strongly-positive vibe anytime I'm in charge. Never show fear in the boat because fear is both irrational and contagious. Also, in the blind, negativity begets negativity, and there is no room for anger in a boat or a blind. I urge my guides to never entertain negativity; we find that it just encourages it. Do not vacillate. Be decisive at all times, courteous and firmly in control of your emotions. Whether people care to admit it or not, they want their boat drivers to be the captains of their vessels. Captaincy abhors a committee. It virtually demands autocraticism, but of course in a positive way.

It's been said that with a perfect guide, a gunner can hunt all day. Then, he does the boat ride back to the dock and the drive back to the hotel. He can have a cocktail, take a shower, consume another cocktail, go to a restaurant, have another cocktail, and then an appetizer and salad. Then it's sometime just before the entrée is served that it dawns on him, "Why, I didn't shoot a thing all day." Now this — *this* — is the perfect guide. Unfortunately, I'm not always that.

It's January 1986. A Nor'easter that forms up off the coast of Cape Canaveral, Florida, a couple days ago finally organizes and strengthens. Near hurricane force northeast gusts directly in our faces become the norm as the day progresses toward evening; thirty-five degrees, horizontal sleet beating our eyeballs mercilessly if we dare look upwind…we don't. Besides, there's no reason to bother looking upwind anyway. Anything pitching into the decoys must come from downwind by aerodynamic necessity, and anything from upwind is moving too fast to hit anyway.

Shooting is great all day. Should have been limited out by nine this morning, but it's two in the afternoon before I realize they're shooting steel number four shot, which is way too light a shot size for all this wind, and their shot pattern in getting blown all to heck. I actually look down one of the man's barrel from behind him as he shoots to finish off a cripple. His shot hits the water three feet to the downwind of where he is aiming! Jeez!

As a result, the few birds that they do manage to hit aren't hit hard, and most manage to flap or flop off downwind for me to try and chase down, off and on all day. Of course, with the wind direction, the water has been blown out of the sound, so all chasing is being done on foot — trudging across the tundra, as I like to call it. We lose a bunch of wounded birds on this day, and that bothers me a lot. I know that nothing in nature gets wasted, but I'm getting kind of cranky anyway. We should be heroes! We should've been limited out with our game straps strained from the weight of good, big ducks and back home napping five hours ago.

I suppose that my disappointment at not having more than four birds in the box, despite shooting a little better than eight boxes of twenty-five shells between them during the course of the day so far, is becoming harder to disguise, especially after the most recent salvo, where yet another flock of a dozen pintail wing off with no dead birds on the water, a straggler losing altitude five hundred yards downwind....

With the cripple chasing and decoy tending I'm having to do all afternoon, I've forgotten to move my boat as the tide has fallen out. Finally able to call the day at sunset, you can imagine my chagrin when I find my boat stuck in shallow water, more like wet sand, actually. I'm only six or seven feet from enough water to float the boat, but push or pull as I might, I can't budge the wench!

Stuck! And the tide won't be dead low for another hour or so. With this wind, it'll take at least two hours after that to get enough water back over the tidal flats to refloat the boat. If these guys want to hit the docks before ten tonight, the boat's got to be floated. NOW!

"Can't. Bad back."

"Me neither. Bad knees."

I am kind of stunned. I've just spent the last twenty minutes pushing, pulling, grunting, rocking and trying to lift and move a twenty-foot fiberglass boat and accompanying forty horsepower outboard motor. Despite the now-freezing temperatures, snow, sleet and now-steady fifty mile per hour winds, with gusts, I'm sweating my butt off.

That each of them would not miss the hundred pounds if they woke up to find one of his hams missing is not lost on me. I'll be the one pushing these guys most of the mile and a half back to the dock.

"Really, I can't even stand for long," says one.

"Truly," says the other "I need to sit down now," he lisps, very Mike Tyson-ish, as his 400 pounds mashes my boat further into the sand. "Do you suppose the restaurant is serving this early? All this fresh air and shooting has me famished."

Up to this point in my life I've had no idea that there is a level beyond incredulous.

"I've ordered a pizza. It's waiting at the dock," is the motivational aid that first springs to mind. Ever cognizant of my tip, I instead interject, "didn't you just hear me say that if we can't move the boat, we're here another three,

maybe four more hours. I've tried, but I can't budge it. My ass is whipped. Being the water's so low we can probably hike home, but it's a few miles, there's some deep spots and I can't carry all of your stuff. We'll probably get wet, but I'm thinking you guys aren't tough enough for that kind of trek anyway."

"Oh, well!" he counters. "If you want to get personal," he sniffs while pushing his girth off the side of the boat.

With that, he walks around to the back of the boat and squats down with his back to the boat's stern. I surmise that a guy's got to have some strong leg muscles to move that much weight around all day, every day. What happens next surprises me, though.

Suddenly he straightens up, pushing the boat's stern with the back of his knees. The boat jumps ahead two feet. He shuffles his feet and repeats the movement and knee-back push. The boat jumps again. Before long, we're afloat.

He rolls into the boat, a big walrus onto a flat rock. His buddy does likewise on the boat's other side.

"What are you waiting for?" he lisps. Their backs to the wind, they're now ready to be pushed home if need be.

Mostly, as it turns out, it does need be.

On a normal day with normal water levels we're only talking a seven-minute boat ride, blind to dock. You've got to know where you're going to stay in the deeper channels, but if you know where to zig and when to zag it's a pretty easy trip. Not so on this night.

I guess the fly in the ointment would focus on how I define "deeper channels." Oregon Inlet on the sound side looks to have wide open waterways. There's water everywhere.

"Just drive, Clive" would seem a good mantra, but that would be incorrect. True, there is water in all directions. It's just that the water in all directions is uniformly really shallow.

Not that we have really extreme tides. We don't. The difference between high and low tides is only eight to ten inches at either end. No. Our problem is that the eight- to ten-inch tide is only augmenting an average water depth of up to your knees here on the tidal flats, but a sufficient wind can move the water up or down another two feet depending on its direction. Tonight, we're a skosh past sufficient....

Oh, and about our deeper channels — they're usually only a few inches to two feet deeper than the rest of the shoals you're driving over. And they're narrow! Maybe five to fifteen yards wide at best. And they don't go straight… unless you expect them not to….

So, here we are: Easily the two largest men I've ever had in my flat-bottomed duck skiff at the same time, dry sand bars all around that are separated by narrow runnels of wind-whipped water that are losing what little depth that they may yet have, blizzard conditions prevailing in the fading light and my two clients are now 800 pounds of recalcitrant dead weight. So what's a guide to do?

Get behind the sleigh and push, is what. Finally, after some angry pushing, I've found water to just below my knees.

Hop into the boat. Release the catch on the motor that allows the motor to tilt up or down. Real quick, I have to jam a chunk of 2 x 6 salt-treated wood between where the motor's stem comes into contact with the boat's stern…Now, I have to digress a moment and admit I saved a few bucks when I decided to purchase this particular motor by opting for, as the salesman put it, the Commercial Model of the motor, the model that has no tilting mechanism…of any kind!

"Save the money," the salesman says. "If you get in shallow water, just tilt the motor forward with one hand and shove your chunk of 2 x 6 up between the motor and the boat with the other, then let go of the motor. Watch your 2 x 6 hand! As the motor falls back into its upright, running position, the motor's stem will bite the chunk of 2 x 6 against the boat's stern, and tilt is achieved."

"Save the money," he says. "A chunk of 2 x 6 works just fine. Save the money. What could be easier?" he says.

Well, maybe spending a little money on a tilting mechanism! The chafe in the shorts of the salesman's plan is that every time you drive tilted-up like this, and your motor touches the bottom, that contact with the bottom makes the motor bounce up just enough to lose the so-called bite the motor has on your chunk of 2 x 6, which at this point falls into the water. Every time!

Now the 2 x 6 needs retrieving, and I'm on the shoal anyway so it's out of the boat and into the darkening gale. I've got to grab my chunk of 2 x 6, re-tilt the motor, set the latch that keeps the motor from falling back on its own and then start pushing. Push till you find infinitesimally deeper water where you start the whole process over again. For all your work you get to putt for about thirty yards before your motor stem contacts the shoal again. Usually though, rather than finding deeper water, you invariably push the boat out of the little runnel you're in. At this point, you have to wander off in different directions until you cipher out where the "deeper" water is.

I'll be honest. These sets of condition almost never come together like this, especially right at dark when you're trying to get home! We're literally involved in a perfect storm scenario. Usually I dream of being out in weather like this because the gunning is quite often fabulous, like today was. Then we all work together and get ourselves home. That's not how this crew wanted to operate.

"We're stuck," I scream over the wail of the wind.

"So?" is the reply.

"So?! So, we've got to find deeper water," I scream back.

"Okay," is the reply.

"Okay? Okay, what?"

"Okay. Go find deeper water."

I'm getting more stunned. I stand there and catch my breath. I puff and wheeze for a good moment, glowering at the now sleet-encrusted lumps sitting stoically, albeit a bit impatiently, for their minion to propel them home. In my brain I'm thinking about how big my tip's going to have to be. Nine boxes of twenty-five shells each box, all fired at good big ducks, and all this pushing. And yet, I can really use some help.

"Could, maybe, like you guys get out of the boat and help me walk it back to the deeper water?"

"Can't," says one.

"Bad back," says the other.

I literally have to push the bow of the boat around to face where we've just come from so that I can then walk around to the stern of the boat, all so that I can now start pushing again to get back to where I was a while ago.

And not just pushing a little bit. Oh, no, no, no. Not so. Think pushing a blocking sled during football practice piled with half of the offensive line. A big offensive line! It's probably the seventh or eighth time that this scenario plays out that I slip over to the dark side.

The dark side: that place where a man or woman finally gets to when normal effort is no longer effective. Think the stereotype of the screaming, invective spewing female in labor. Yeah, that place! That place wherein Satan dwells in evilness and doles out energy only if you come over to his side.

When reason and goodness have failed, therein lurks Satan. His residence is in a place wherein men or women can — and do — string together fifteen epithets, in unique combinations, that are full of insightful, colloquially intriguing, anatomical possibility. These strings of cursing emerge under my breath as I set my feet under myself immediately prior to the drive that is required to push a fully-loaded boat the thirty yards back to where I just was — all so I can start all over again in a different direction.

An hour has elapsed as this scenario repeats itself over and over. Not only is a steady stream of imaginative cursing now flowing freely from the depths of my soul, just prior to another screaming push, but I'm also now laughing at myself intermittently due to the absurdity of the entirety of my solo effort. Occasionally I bite at the sleet for good measure. It's possible that I may be suffering the effects of an endorphin overdose.

If God were a British fellow and He was taking time off from doing God Stuff to observe the last hour of the skinny duck guide pushing the boat full of recalcitrant large dudes all across Oregon Inlet, during a blizzard and in the dark, all by himself, he'd have to opine, "Why, I do believe the young lad's gone quite wonky! I don't blame him, really."

With all of this, however, I still believe that my tip for the day is safe. "Just another guide doing whatever it takes to get his clients to the dock at the end of a long day," I imagine to myself. Par for the course on this day of days, I'm wrong again. Looking back on it, however, I don't think anything I've done just yet has cost me my tip.

The end of my ordeal is at hand, but I'm at an impasse. I've finally pushed around a couple of low islands to the end of the shoals. All I have left to do is to push the boat into the deeper channel, jump in, release the tilted motor, let it fall back to the upright position, pull-start the engine, pull-tilt the motor forward, shove the chunk of 2 x 6 between motor and stern, put the motor in gear and then putt the last half-mile to the dock.

Except that every time I try to execute said sequence, at exactly the moment where I put the motor in gear to putt to the dock, the incoming tide and wind push the boat back onto the shoal, the motor touches bottom, the chunk of 2 x 6 falls out and the motor stem pins us on the shoal...again and again. Aaaaaggggh!

I've attempted the final escape sequence six times in a row with the same results: push boat into deeper water, jump in, release tilt, engine falls back to the upright position, pull-start engine, pull-tilt motor forward, 2 x 6 under motor stem, in gear, get pushed back on shoal, hit bottom, chunk of 2 x 6 falls in water, stuck. Repeat. I try once again for help.

"Look. Could one of you hold the boat for...."

"Can't"

"Bad back."

"Yeah, yeah. I know. Bad knees."

A derisive snort is all the help I can expect — and then... out of nowhere...the proverbial final straw.

"Give me a life jacket!" spoken as an imperial command from Mr. Bad Back.

"What?!" I nearly shout, my head snapping around to look the man in the eyes.

"Give me a life jacket," is the reply.

"Are you serious? You can't be serious!" I now scream in my best John McEnroe voice.

"You never know," is the reply.

"What do you mean, you never know? Didn't you just sit there for the last hour and watch me run all over, in every direction, in ankle deep water?"

"You never know," the rote response.

I cease pushing for a moment — and a moment is all it takes for the boat to reverse its forward momentum and to drift past me with the wind and tide pushing it. I never lose eye contact with Bad Back as he drifts past me in the boat and again ends up on the shoal. Diplomacy enters my mind...I reject it.

"Sir," I say as he drifts by me. I grab the life jacket on which he's sitting as he goes by. I hear a satisfying thunk as his rump hits the wet seat when I snatch it out from under him, four hundred pounds and all.

"Sir," I continue as I thrust the life jacket into his arms. I punctuate every syllable slowly.

"SIR, I WOULD HAVE TO KNOCK YOU OUT OF THIS BOAT. THEN I'D HAVE TO STAND ON YOUR HEAD. AND THEN I'D HAVE TO POUR WATER UP YOUR NOSE FOR YOU TO DROWN TONIGHT!"

Then my head whips around to survey his startled companion — I growl at him…a good, low growl of satisfying duration.

I mutter under my breath as I grab and swing the stern around and into the wind, loud enough to hear, but too worn out to give a whit. "Oh, we don't want to hold the boat? No problem. No. No. It's okay. I've got it. You, save your back. And you...you save your knees. No, no. You just sit, I've got it."

All the while I've pushed the boat stern — first off the shoals as deep as I dare. I jump in. Snatch the engine alive and before we're blown back onto the shoal, I kick the engine into gear, but this time into reverse gear.

Before my boys can react, I duck down and behind my motor and gun the engine. Where Bad Knees and Bad Back have had their backs to the wind for most of the trip, the spray and sleet has rolled harmlessly off them. Now, we're going full-throttle in reverse and into the winds…This game has just taken a very interesting turn. My boys are all of a sudden face-to-face with the full fury of the storm.

Each wave that slaps the stern of the boat leaps immediately upward and then the seventy-mile-an-hour wind gusts catch the airborne wave and drive the water mercilessly and cruelly into my guys' unprotected faces and down their collars. You've got to picture it: I'm literally hiding down behind the motor so all the waves go over my head and combine with the horizontally driven sleet to slam into their fleshy white faces at speeds matching the wind's near hurricane force.

Ahhh…this is very satisfying for me. I near about swamp my boat, racing sternward into the tempest, all the while hiding behind my motor and watching their faces as they take pelting wave after pelting wave. I race in reverse long enough to ensure that they get soaked, through their collars, clean down to their undershorts. Only then do I spin the boat around and head for the docks, albeit at a speed slow enough to ensure that all that salt spray that ran down their jackets' neck has had enough time to trickle down their chests and eventually to pool under their ample briskets. Now…I am happy.

I'm pretty much sure that it was right about there that I lost my tip that night, but man, the looks in their eyes and the sounds of the squishing in their boots as they waddled off to their car once we got to the dock made me very, very, happy.

YOU BRING THE WEATHER

Photo courtesy Troy Cranford.

Newcomers to our guide service regularly ask when is the best time to hunt on the Outer Banks of North Carolina. My answer is always the same. The only sure correlation to good gunning is good "ducky" weather — cold, with a vengeful low pressure system whipping into town should be your holy grail. Blizzards work well, too, but coastal Nor'easters are the best. North winds of any degree work wonders. Northeast, northwest, or dead on north...it does not seem to matter. We just need north wind — lots of it — and a falling barometer. Fifteen to twenty-five mph is good, but twenty-five to thirty with gusts over forty is better. Low clouds are a must, and off and on drizzle/snow/sleet makes our world come to life. These magic days are not for the faint-hearted, however.

One year we got back-to-back blizzards. We got the second blizzard day late in January, on the twentieth if I'm not mistaken. When we pull into the docks — in the dark after our hunt that day — we are met by one of our state Wildlife Officers. He makes sure all of us know that he has spent the afternoon observing us from a clandestine location. Then he opens up a bit more than I expect him to.

"Man, you guys were really out there. I mean, I can't believe you guys could hang in that gale! What an awesome bunch of blinds you have!" I answer with a wearied, knowing look and a quick laugh. The officer continues, "Dag! That was bunches of pintail. How do you keep your guys from shooting into all those flocks of pintail?"

A little indignantly I say, "I tell them not to."

He: "Oh, so you can tell them in time?"

Me: "Well, of course. It's my job, and it saves you a lot of time not writing the tickets."

He, satisfied: "Man, you guys were right in the teeth of that blizzard. You know there were gusts over sixty? How could you guys even stand the wind chill and sleet out there?"

Me: "Really good clothes and 1600 milligrams of thinsulate on your feet."

Oh, and keep your back to it. Any bird has to land into that much wind. Who cares what's going on upwind. You'd never hit it, anyway. Yeah, that was about as extreme as anything I've been out in for a while. One time we were trying to finish off a wounded bird and I'm telling the guys, "When he swims into that open spot between the decoys, lay him out." He swims into the open and both guys' guns go off at the same time. Ba-Blam! And both their charges hit a foot and a half to the downwind of the bird. The wind blew their shot a foot and a half off-target over a span of forty yards! Oh yeah, I say, half under my breath, we missed bunches. Bunches of bunches as a matter of fact. Man, what a day!

What a day! I hunt fifty-five to sixty days a year just so I can be there on that one day — but I don't know what day it'll be till after it's happened. Some years you have five or seven of those days, and other years you may not have any. So, in answer to your question: Any time is the best time to gun the Outer Banks, but if you want *THAT* day, you'll have to bring us *THAT* weather.

A MARRY-ABLE DEVELOPMENT

I will have to say this for my sweetie (whom I married a quarter-century ago): Ellen is not shy about jumping right into the middle of any project that needs doing in relation to the guide business — and she'll bring enough food to feed anybody associated with the project as well.

Photo courtesy Troy Cranford.

No kidding! Ellen has cleaned all the ducks for entire seasons. She's answered the phones and booked decades' worth of clients for countless guides. She books rooms, organizes game dinners at a local restaurant, paints decoys, helps build blinds, and has lugged enough brush to camouflage a boat-hide big enough to hide an aircraft carrier.

My wife is so inclined to pitch in that I need to keep an extra wary eye to protect her from herself. It's in the core of her nature to walk up to a project, assess the scenario, and then grab the heaviest object in sight and lug it until she either gets it where it needs to go or she injures herself… if she doesn't injure herself on the first trip, she'll repeat the maneuver until she has or the project gets finished. There's an example of this that happened back before we were married that still gives me the willies whenever I think about it.

In those days, our camouflage of choice to hide our duck blinds was sedge. For those of you who are unfamiliar, sedge is a single stalked plant that stands about eight to ten feet tall. The entire plant consists of the single, bamboo-like stem and long, slender, oppositely occurring leaves that grow upwardly and wrapped around the stem until they eventually fall away and arc into space. Sedge looks kind of like a leafier cattail, but without the cattails…and earlier, when I compared the sedge stem to bamboo, I may have misled.

A sedge stem is much more brittle and splintery than a bamboo stem and it doesn't get nearly as thick as does bamboo. Fully grown, sedge is about ten feet tall with a stem about as big around as a man's thumb. When you harvest sedge, you usually cut it about eight to ten inches above where it enters the ground. Depending on how you cut the sedge stems, the resulting stubs are either sharpened like a punji stick or they're a jaggedly splintered, ten-inch tall, straight, limb-like remainder sticking out of the ground. Each plant grows no more than six inches away from the next plant so, after harvest, the shoreline you just whacked down is an expanse of eight-inch stubs sticking out of the ground.

The chore of harvesting sedge is made even more menacing by virtue of the fact that each sedge leaf is about twelve inches long, but extremely tough, yet slender on either edge, and seems to have been invented solely to inflict wicked paper-like cuts upon the bare flesh of any human foolish enough to get near them.

We used up truckloads upon truckloads of sedge every year to hide our blinds and over time developed a fairly effective means of harvest that enabled us to cut, bundle, and haul copious amounts of the unwieldly grass in short amounts of time. The operation required at least four people to do it right.

The first guy was the sedge cutter. When we first began harvesting sedge, we'd cut each stalk individually with a sharp implement. This is the method of harvest that yields the acres of punji stick strewn shoreline when you're done. This also took forever.

We soon learned that if you took a small chain saw, you could rev the bad boy up and, by bending at the waist and swinging the saw in a sweeping motion, you could cut whole swathes of sedge. If you entered a stand of sedge and started cutting with a swinging motion that was consistently in the same direction, you could cut an ever-growing circle of sedge that always fell in the same direction. Kind of like a crop circle.

This made the second person's job easier because they were the bundler. The bundler's job was to grab an armload of sedge that was all aimed the same way (tops all on one end and bottoms all on the other) and cinch and tie the bundle in two places about five feet apart with heavy twine.

The other two people were the haulers, and their job was to grab the bundles and haul them out of the marsh one by one.

All three jobs were brutal in their own way, but each was also universally agonizingly hot and sweaty due to the fact that the job had to be done before the gunning season began and that was early in the fall while it was still warm out. Before long, each person would be sedge paper-cut on just about any unclothed flesh and sweating copiously under any flesh that was clothed to protect you from the sedge cuts.

Like any group of peons engaged in manual labor of this odious nature, you tend to fall into a zombie-like persona as you endure your tasks as best you can. Your only glimmer of hope lies in getting the vehicles loaded to capacity and strapped down for the drive to the boat ramp.

The drive to the boat ramp was your only break. When you got there, all the sedge bundles needed to be unloaded from the vehicles and heaped onto boats for the ride to the duck blinds that needed brushing. If you got enough people lined up to work, you could get all facets of the job working at the same time, so at the end of a long day, you could get two or three blinds brushed in a day. Each blind to be brushed consumed twelve to fifteen good-sized bundles of sedge to make it properly disappear.

So, here we all were, peons bent to our tasks, enduring our particular travails in sweaty sedge-sliced silence. We had Ellen's two boys, both shy of ten years, myself, Ellen, her brother, a couple of the guides, my ex-brother-in-law/good buddy from New York City, my red-neck buddy, Ross, and several other friends who would like to be considered whenever I had an open day that coincided with some duck-nasty weather.

I'd been running the chain saw, Ellen's youngest son had been tying up the bundles, and Ellen, her older son, and Ross had been hauling the bundles and stacking them on the empty boat trailer that we'd been utilizing as a transport vehicle. We'd all been working a few hours and had already hauled two full loads of sedge to the boat ramp where the other guys had been doing the boating and brushing of the blinds.

We're just about a half-hour into gathering our third and final trailer load when Ellen trudged past me with a full bundle in tow. At first, I admired her tenacity and how well she was getting around in the old pair of hip boots of mine that were four sizes too big for her more feminine feet.

She had already passed before it dawned on me that something didn't seem quite right. Was I getting delirious from the heat and gas fumes, or was Ellen stuffing her shirttail up her nose when she walked by? Perplexed, I shut down the chain saw.

"Ellen," I called out, a bit too loudly for the close quarters of the little cut-over we were both toiling in. I was used to the incessant scream of the chain saw, and I was overcompensating now that I'd shut it off. More volume-appropriate, "Ellen, are you okay?" She didn't seem to want to turn toward me or respond, so I followed after her and gently turned her toward me with a hand on her shoulder.

When she finally did turn toward me, I was surprised to see tears running down her cheeks and blood on her shirttail.

"Hey…hey! What's going on?" I asked, very concerned.

"I tripped in a nutria hole," was all she'd say. She shrugged my hand off her shoulder so she wouldn't lose her momentum with the sedge bundle. I followed her to where the truck and trailer were parked before she'd let loose of the takes-both-arms-to-reach-around and ten-foot-long bundle.

"Okay now, out with it," I demanded, "that's too much blood for the sedge cuts and what's up with the crying? Did you sprain your ankle when you tripped? You're not limping," I noted with exasperation. "I can't help you with anything if I don't know what it is. I'm not going to leave you alone until you tell me," I added for good measure.

"Okay, okay," she finally sighed as she tried to dab at the inside of her nose again where a persistent trickle of blood kept reforming between dabs with her shirttail. "I was just getting a bundle of sedge moving…."

"When?"

"When, what?" she asked.

"When…this bundle?"

"No, about three bundles ago," she answered. "Anyway, I was pulling and tugging on the bundle to separate it from another bundle that it'd gotten hung up with, and you know how, once you get it moving, you don't want to stop because you'll have to get it moving again if you do stop," she explained, all in one breath. "Just when the two bundles separated, I got an extra two steps of speed and right then stepped into the stupid rat hole and pitched forward as I fell," she finished while staring down at the clown-sized boots that she'd had to borrow to even help us in the first place.

"So what happened to your nose? Did you hit it on the ground when you fell?" I asked. I was concerned that I'd asked a girl to do more than I should have and had worked her too hard. I grabbed the bundle that she'd just drug to the truck and started to heave it onto the top of the sedge pile atop the trailer when she added a final detail to the end of her account that froze me in mid-heave.

"When I pitched forward after stepping into the nutria hole, a stub of sedge got rammed up my nose before I hit the ground," she finished as she dabbed daintily at her still oozing nose.

"What?" My knees almost buckled from the image as it flashed through my brain. "You mean one of the cut-off stubs that are sticking out of the ground?"

"Yeah," under her breath.

"Three bundles ago?"

"Um-hmm. Maybe four, I can't be sure."

"So you're telling me that you tripped, fell, and the only thing that kept your face from hitting the ground was the raggedy, jaggedy, chainsaw-cut sedge stub that got jammed up your nose."

"Um-hmm," she sighed in agreement.

"Wasn't it splintery? You're lucky you didn't get splinters inside your nose."

"Oh, those," she acknowledged, "I've already pulled about six or seven of those out."

"Of your nose!"

"Yeah, what else are you going to do? You can't leave them in there or they'll fester," she answered matter-of-factly. My knees almost buckled again. "Let's get back to work," she added. "If you're not cutting, everybody's got to stop."

"You jammed a splintery sedge butt up your nose, pulled out six or seven of the splinters from inside your nose, and now you want to get back to work?" I dropped the bundle of sedge that I was still holding onto and stood there with my hands on my hips and wondered to myself how big a baby I'd have been if I'd done the same thing to my nose. I got a wave of the willies just thinking about it.

I just got another wave of the willies writing about it better than a quarter-century later.

I was really hanging suspended from the horns of a dilemma at this point. I wasn't sure whether to run away and be very, very afraid of the small Irish woman standing before me so stoically in her too-big-boots with sedge cuts festooned on her exposed arms and hands and her nose oozing blood from the sedge splinters she'd pulled from inside her nose — or to propose marriage forthwith.

I really didn't see there being any other options than those two…I just knew that, if it ever came to it, I wanted her on my team.

Italian Venison SANDWICHES

There's nothing better to come home to after a day of brushing blinds than the following recipe. Also, it's so easy to just throw everything in a crock pot in the morning and come home to a house that smells wonderful and have a meal that's all ready for a hungry crew to boot.

INGREDIENTS:
4-lb. venison ham (or two small shoulders, deboned)
2-3 Anaheim peppers, cored and thinly sliced
1 sweet red or yellow pepper, cored and sliced
1 green pepper, cored and sliced
1 Vidalia onion, peeled and sliced
1 stick butter
4 cups water
3 beef bouillon cubes
1 pkg. beef au jus
1-2 tablespoons oregano
5 cloves garlic, finely diced
2 teaspoons black pepper
6-8 pepperoncini plus one tablespoon of the juice (These are found next to the pickles and olives at your grocers, they are also called Tuscon peppers.)
2 loaves crusty French bread
1 pkg. Provolone cheese slices

Load into crock pot in order given. Cook on high for 5-6 hours or low for eight hours. Shred meat using two knives, scissor fashion. Slice bread lengthwise, top with cheese slices. Pop in a 375-degree oven till cheese melts. Remove. Pile high with shredded meat and peppers, spooning au jus over top. Serve with additional au jus for dipping, if desired. Add a nice potato salad and some sliced tomatoes with fresh mozzarella and balsamic vinaigrette and you're ready for a hungry crowd!

SLOW DAY STRATEGY

This being the forty-second anniversary of my first day as a duck guide, I feel qualified to offer some predictions regarding what is about to transpire prior to each new fowling season. Of course, predictions are only guesses and should be held to the same standards as are the yearly prognostications put forth by weather gurus concerning future hurricane activity.

Photo courtesy Troy Cranford.

In short, what meteorologists and an experienced duck guide have in common in their attempts to predict future weather is their sharing of pure intellectual folly. What's going to happen will happen, no matter how hard we try to will events to our benefit. The exception to this, of course, is Pat Robertson. I guess when you're that tight with the Supreme Being, you have privileges.

Successful water fowling is not nearly as much determined by a full bag limit as it is with camaraderie and lasting memories. A full bag will feed you for a few days, but potent visuals and shared memories will sustain you for a lifetime, or at least, hopefully, into your dotage.

In my mind, when you're old and in the nursing home, your memories are going to be more to your benefit than your saved dollars. A bed is a bed...I'm just saying.

CRAZY CHESSIES

Chesapeake retriever dogs are known for their wackiness. They've achieved this distinction honestly.

They're really clever and smart to a fault. Fairly bursting with energy, they can be a handful. Now, add in a near manic desire to involve themselves into anything their owner is doing and (dare I say) pure doggedness. Finally, mix in some very real trust issues (both positive and negative), and you may begin to catch a drift of the challenges that lie ahead for a Chesapeake Bay retriever dog owner.

Photo courtesy Troy Cranford.

Oh, yeah. They also seem to have a wicked sense of humor…particularly with their poop. Gabby was the best dog I've ever had, but whenever you'd get settled in to hunt she'd drop a stinker straight up wind — or she'd mine your only path into or out of your gunning spot — and then she'd sit back with that big Chesapeake grin on her face and wait.

Never confuse this breed with any other retriever dogs, Labs in particular. Labs are happy to let humans be the boss. They actually believe that you, the human, know what's best. Heck, they'll do as they're told without even bothering to ever think about it.

A Chesapeake retriever dog will never take what you say at face value. Anything coming out of your mouth is questionable at best, yet nonetheless it gets filtered through what they'd prefer to be doing at that particular moment in time. This is why if you are ever going to successfully train a Chessy to do anything, you're going to have to take the time to convince them that, whatever you want them to do, is what they wanted to do in the first place. I am not kidding.

And, make no mistake — this dog is trying to train you just as hard as you're trying to train him or her. No, that's incorrect. They're trying harder to train you! They're twenty-four/seven to your two/five or six. Once again, I'm not kidding.

Give Labradors their due. You can get them started just about right out of the crate. They learn quickly. It's not at all uncommon for a lab to be hunting fairly well at eight months, polished at a year and a half. Not so, the curly-haired brown dog. Rather, if you don't know this breed's nuances, they're very often ruined by eight months and a menace at a year and a half!

I believe the pivotal difference in the two is what I mentioned earlier, the part about having to take the time to make the dog think that what you want him/her to do is what the dog wanted to do in the first place. This, in addition to a lack of maturity, is literally why it takes twice as long to train this breed.

Having said all of that, however, I'd have to follow that observation and aver that their weakness is also their strong suit. You see, if you put in the time up-front and let the dog think that he/she is training you all along…well, in the end,

you've got a partner that really believes in what they're doing! And, why not? If done right, it's their idea in the first place.

At this point you really begin to hunt together.

Whistles? You don't need no stinking whistles!

Just talk to the beast. They know what you want because they want it too. Besides, a Chesapeake's natural hunting instincts are easily superior to whatever you may think you know about retrieving. Just get 'em near (downwind) of where a bird went down, then get out of their way…and don't stink up the lie. Dag, but it's beautiful watching a Chessy cipher out a double blind retrieve.

Anyway, the long and short of it is that I'm a Chesapeake guy. My Dad had 'em as far back as I can remember, quite literally, as a matter of fact.

I remember being on a road trip with the whole family, and the four of us kids were supposed to be asleep in the back of our VW van. Of course the dogs were sleeping in the same pile as we were. I was maybe four of five. Even Mom was napping in the front seat. I was wiggling around too much to suit our male dog, Thor. (I know. Us kids had found out that we had a Norwegian heritage and all fancied ourselves to be descendants of Vikings — hence the name Thor.) I must have inadvertently elbowed the dog in the ribs or something because, all of a sudden, danged if he didn't grab me by the shoulder and growl. Not hard enough to hurt me or leave a mark, but plenty enough to let me know to knock it off.

I couldn't believe it. Even in my little boy's brain I knew that I was supposed to be the superior being. In my mind I assessed my position.

I can wiggle if I want to! He's the pet, I reasoned to myself. And I'm the human! I wiggled again.

In an instant, Thor had me by the shoulder again. This time the growl was lower and more drawn out. The implication was clear. I needed back-up!

"Dad!" I screamed, "Thor, bit me."

"What do you mean?" He sounded more exasperated than concerned. He knew that our Chessies were too protective of us kids to do any real harm. "Are you hurt?"

He couldn't turn his head to check things out as, at the time, he was negotiating traffic around New York City at dusk. He had timed the trip so we'd arrive at Grandma and Grandpa's house in Mastic Beach on Long Island in time for dinner. Even back in 1961 the traffic around the city was sixty to sixty-five miles an hour and bumper to bumper.

"No," I replied less stridently, "but he's a bad dog!"

"Well, did he bite you or not?"

I warmed to my sense of inter-species social injustice again. I started to put the wail back into my voice.

"I just moved around a little bit and he didn't like it. He grabbed my shoulder...and he growled!" I was about to tear up at the thought of being bossed around by the family pet. It's bad enough that my sister got to torture me just because she's a girl. I was prepared to draw the line at answering to the dogs too. The injustice!

"So, there's no blood," my Dad ascertained with a quick glance over his shoulder.

"No," I whimpered back, sniffling for effect.

"Well, then, do what he wants," came the startling reply. "We told you half an hour ago to go to sleep."

"But..." was my surprised response.

"No buts!" Vern was never one to not recognize an opportunity when one presented itself in raising us four kids. He also never failed to teach.

"You kids and the dogs are a pack and, sorry, but he's superior to you."

This shocked me to my bones, him siding with the dog and all, but before I could mount any type of prolonged protest, he continued.

"And no wonder, he outweighs you and he's pretty sure he's smarter, too."

A shocked holler began to build and threatened to awaken the whole bus. Before that could happen, my Dad quickly restored peace and quiet with his next revelation.

"Look! If Thor thinks he's the boss, nothing else matters. Right now he is the boss unless you're willing to fight him for it. And you'll have to win...." He let that trail ominously. "If he wants to bite you right now, I can't stop him without wrecking the car and killing everybody in it."

I couldn't help it. That made good sense.

"What you're going to have to do right now is whatever he wants. Tomorrow we can work on how you can be his boss, but right now, you're on your own." Then he added, "If Thor wants you still and quiet, I'd suggest you stay real still...and real quiet!"

"What?!" I fairly shriek. I spin to get a better look at my Dad to see how serious he really was.

I didn't get to finish the spin though, because, I was sure, the dog was somehow emboldened by what my Dad had just said. He had me by the arm again, and this time, I was sure that the growl was, at best, a precursor... so...like any underling in any pack would do, I froze and didn't move again till I fell asleep.

I guess my fate was sealed that night. I had to learn how to work with these dogs or I'd be the bitch forever. I mean, I kind of had to. I figure along the way I ended up a Chesapeake guy.

As the van became quiet again on that long ago road trip, I learned something else. An even more poignant lesson dawned on me as I heard my Dad mutter under his breath as he was once again able to focus on the hellish traffic that was all trying to circumvent driving through New York City at the same time. A beast can be your ally in many circumstances... The last thing I heard as I fell into a subdued sleep: "Good dog, Thor. Good dog."

NATURE/ NURTURE REVISITED

I graduated college with a biology/philosophy double major. My favorite biology professor was a bird guy. No matter the course title, the science involved was bird related. If your course title said "Endocrinology," it was actually going to be the endocrinology of birds. "Bacteriology" would be the bacteriology of birds and so on. He frequently became frustrated with me for my anthropomorphizing nature (the giving of human attributes to nature's flora and fauna).

Photo courtesy Vic Berg.

"Victor," singling me out, "why is the Spartina grass tallest in the intertidal zone?"

"Because it's happier there," I'd answer.

"No, no! Grasses can't be happy," he'd correct.

"Of course they can. The Spartina in the intertidal zone get better nutrients so they grow larger than their peers. Necessarily, they'll have bigger, stronger root systems and, as such, they're allowed more space per plant. Be honest. You'd be happier too if you had more to eat, got it easier, had a bigger yard, and were, deductively, way more successful at breeding." I pause to give him time to succumb to my reasoning. Instead....

"Aaagh. Grass can't make all the decisions you've attributed to it. You've got all the facts right except that nature doesn't think."

I'm pretty sure that he's being intractable.

"Okay Vic," he'd try again, "why do the periwinkle snails crawl up the Spartina grass stalks? One would think that would make them prone to predation."

"Easy. They don't like the water and they're not afraid of the Marsh hens."

"What?"

"They can't hold their breath for long while underwater, and the glue that connects and holds them to their environment doesn't do so well when soaked. Of course, then, they don't like water and strive to avoid it by climbing the only things around, the Spartina grasses." I continue, imagining myself to be quite the scholar, "Once up there, though, they're exposed to being eaten, mostly by Marsh hens — excuse me — Clapper Rails. The snails don't need to worry though, because their house is indigestible and the Marsh hens — Clapper Rails — would rather eat something that doesn't consist of three-quarters indigestible material. You've got to imagine that the poops would be pretty brutal as well."

"Aagh! Strive to avoid...worry...their house...would rather...brutal poops... Aaaagh!"

He never succeeded in curing me of my anthropomorphizing nature. Bless his heart. He tried, but I still can't see critters as genetically mandated automatons. I've watched critters cipher.

The scientific dogma is that nature's critters can't figure stuff out on their own, that all of their behavior is instinctual. They can be taught, but they can't think for themselves.

Yeah, right. See, I don't buy into that theory so much. To be honest, I spend a lot more time in nature than my professor ever did and I'm in on nature's misguiding secret. Critters are always thinking.

Spend a lifetime partnering up with the curly-haired brown dogs and see how you feel after spending significant time with them. They can't think for themselves? Yeah, right. I tell the next story to highlight the breed's toughness and independent nature.

Willy, Ward's Surf Dog

Back in the days when surfers were our beach's predominant year-round residents, we were all young and lived to surf.

For employment, we about all fell into two industries: service or construction and their trades. In general, the service workers were night owls and construction guys early risers. In those days, each group's work schedule allowed for surf breaks sometime during any day that the waves were good. You probably couldn't surf all day, but you could surf every day for a couple hours.

On a strong surf day you'd very often see different surf breaks dominated by different construction crews. If the lead guy of a crew was taking a two-hour, hot time of the day surf break to cool off with a few waves, the rest of his crew was usually in the lineup as well.

I'll never forget the day when my wife's brother, Ed, moved to the beach from Chicago, Illinois. One of the things Ed brought with him from the Midwest was a well-developed work ethic.

We were driving down the beach and showing Ed around right after his arrival from Chicago. In those days, there was a lot of construction going on. After passing our fifth job site, Ed had a quizzical look in his eyes.

"Is today a holiday?" he asked.

"No. Why do you ask?"

"Well, we just drove by five job sites and nobody was working at any of them.

"Oh, there's surf today," Ellen and I answered matter-of-factly and in unison. We thought Eddy was going to have a stroke. The very idea: that work on the entire beach would come to a screeching halt just because there were waves! Which, I'm going to insist, brings us to Ward's Chessy, Willy. I only tell this story to attest to the character of these beasts.

Back in those days, every young male surfer had three things: a rusty four-wheel-drive pick-up truck, a surf board on the rack atop its roof and a big dog in the passenger seat. Your dog went everywhere you went, no exceptions.

On every job site every morning and out the back door of every restaurant at night, there'd be three or four big dogs nosing around and waiting for their bosses to get off work.

After the required butt sniffing and jockeying about rituals were performed, most of the dogs ended up asleep underneath or in the front seat of "their" trucks with the door wide open. There was no need to lock the trucks because nobody was getting past the dog.

My buddy Wardy had a big Chesapeake male named Willy. Wardy never duck hunted, but he was as big of a surf bum as any of the rest of us. It's too bad Willy never got a chance to hunt as he'd have been a natural. You could always tell when Wardy's crew was surfing because Willy would be out there with them! On really big surf days, too. Ward tried to keep Willy on the beach, but Willy was relentless and would usually escape whatever ploy Ward would concoct to keep him out of the surf. You couldn't leave that dog in any truck because he'd eat it — the inside of the truck, I mean: seats, headrests, gear-shift knob, door panels, tool belts, rain coats…you get the drift.

I remember many days when I'd be sitting out past the end of the fishing piers with Wardy, waiting for the next line of waves to arrive from some far off hurricane. Big waves, too! They had fifteen- to twenty-foot faces on average. Invariably, we'd glance back to the beach and Wardy would cuss under his breath. There, clearing the last of the whomping shore break, would be Willy, dog-paddling stoically along, impervious to the big wave pummeling, looking for his boss. Where surfers sit while they wait for their next wave is called the lineup. The lineup is the area just beyond where the biggest waves break, and the water's surface in this area is surprisingly calm. Once the dog had found Wardy, he was happy to paddle around and visit with all us other surfers. Any time the dog would get tired, he'd simply commandeer the nearest surfer's surfboard. No, really! Willy'd just swim right up to you and drape himself across your surfboard. Of course, you'd get unbalanced from the dog climbing onto your board and you'd fall off — and there was nothing you could do about it. Willy was a BIG Chessy. If you tried to push him off and get your board back, you'd get growled and snapped at for your troubles. You really couldn't do anything but tread water until Willy was rested and swam off on his own.

Geez, it was hilarious: some self-obsessed, would-be surf superstar treading water and cussing Willy while the rest of us surfed and laughed…until Willy ran you off of your board on a triple overhead day and while a set wave was bearing down on you. Then it was your turn to tread water and cuss the dog.

Back in the '80s, there was a legendary Chessy in the Florida Keys. The bar where his boss hung out sat alongside a 25-foot-deep lagoon. For entertainment, the dog would dare bar patrons to throw a painted rock into the lagoon. You got it. The crazy Chessy would dive to the bottom and retrieve it. He'd do it all day if you'd let him.

YOU KNOW YOU'RE IN TROUBLE WHEN THE DOG CAN COUNT

Yoda was my first Chesapeake. I got her right after I graduated college and moved to the beach full-time. The dog really wasn't an option, as back then every young male had a rusted 4 x 4 pickup truck, a surf board or three, and a big dog. Please note that a girlfriend was not a constant in this equation.

Photo taken by Richard Darcy, Courtesy Vic Berg.

During duck season I guided or hunted every day of the week but Sunday. Months on end, Yoda was my constant companion. She was consumed with hunting ducks and imbued with an intense tenacity for the occupation as a water fowl retrieval specialist. It had long ago been established that, as she could not tell me how to shoot the ducks, I was similarly not to bother her with my opinions concerning retrieval issues.

Our arrangement was simple: My jobs were, in Yoda's mind, to do the decoys, shoot the ducks — while never missing — and then to get us home where Ellen could then feed her. Her jobs, on the other hand, were to stare at the sky and wish the very ducks into existence and then to retrieve and store all the downed fowl.

For her efforts, Yoda demanded (and received) twenty percent of anything I ate during the day while afield. This reminds me of the time, after a pitiful spate of begging and drooling, I dropped a raw oyster onto her outstretched tongue. She didn't know what to do with the slimy rascal. The look in her eyes was hilarious. As much as she loved to eat — I don't think she even knew how to not swallow food — I swear that raw oyster sat on her tongue for tens of seconds before she finally figured how to spit it out...but that's another story.

As I implied earlier, I wasn't to annoy the dog with silly rules. We humans were to shoot the fowl and the dog was to go and get it. Simple, no commands, and certainly no whistles! Absolutely no micro-managing the dog was to be tolerated or, swear to God, she'd hard-mouth the next ten birds that she retrieved. You humans just keep your butts in the blind and shoot more ducks was the unwritten law. There was no reason for a human to even pick up a fowl unless it needed to be humanely dispatched.

The final result of this arrangement was that Yoda made her own pile of retrieved birds nearby wherever she chose to sit that day. If you did need to dispatch a wounded bird, you were supposed to give it back to her so that she could then put it onto her pile. She kept track.

She made danged sure that all birds ended up on her pile, even if she had to sneak into the blind and steal it off of the blind's seat. She would not be denied. If a gunner wanted to keep a bird nice for mounting he'd be allowed to arrange it the way he wanted, but he'd have to leave it outside of the blind, and on her pile.

This was back in the days of three bird limits per man so it wasn't all that unusual to limit out and have to quit gunning early. This never sat well with Yoda. Things would be going great. We'd be crushing ducks and then we'd quit...Just like that, we'd pick up the decoys and go home. In Yoda's mind, quitting under these circumstances was just wrong!

Well, it's not long before the dog figures out a way to keep us gunning longer. When we are getting near our limit and not paying attention, Yoda would hide some of our ducks. This almost always would include the nice mounters that the guys were most interested in getting home to their taxidermists.

It wasn't like she'd do it all the time, and the frequency of limiting out wasn't all that high, so she almost always caught me off-guard with this particular gambit. She hid them good, too! You could spend a lifetime looking, but you'd never be able to find where the ducks got tucked under a clump of marsh grass. I guess the first couple times she pulled this stunt we didn't help ourselves by staying to try to replace the birds that she'd "lost."

I mean, you try explaining to a couple of guys from Ohio that the bull pintails with the eleven-inch sprigs that they'd been dreaming of shooting and mounting all of their lives were gone and there was no way the danged dog was going to show you where she hid them...at least not until all the decoys, clients, and all their stuff was in the boat and she was sure that we were heading home. Only then, would she disappear — and soon reappear — with one of the trophy birds in her mouth.

Until I caught on to the fact that the knuckle-headed dog could count and would forestall our departure by hiding fowl, I was faced with a series of tough calls.

"Nice shot!" I'd say, satisfied. "That should do us. A nice limit of birds! Let's get this mess picked up and head for home...Shoot!?!"

"What's the matter?"

"There should be nine ducks here. Where're your pintails? Yoda!"

"Is there a problem?" the clients ask again, worry in their voices. "You told us to leave the birds on the dog's pile or else she'd keep stealing them and putting them there anyway." Now, nearly hysterical, "We waited all our lives and drove a long way to shoot those pintails. We're not leaving without them."

What I have to say next isn't very reassuring.

"I'm pretty sure Yoda just doesn't want us to quit hunting," I try to explain. "If we pick up the decoys and load up the boat, I'm pretty sure she'll bring them out when she's sure that we're really going to go."

This was followed by a prolonged, awkward silence as how lame that sounded registers with me. I can do the math. It'd take at least forty-five minutes to get all the decoys up and the boat loaded. If at that point the idiot dog still wouldn't produce their trophies, I'd have to put the decoys back out and, besides looking like a dog-whipped lug-nut, we'd have wasted an hour and a half. The real rub in the ointment, though, is that I don't doubt that the dog could tell if I tried bluffing.

Invariably, around that time, I'd see a group of pintail in the air. Long story short: I let the guys shoot replacement trophies. I kind of had to, even though, at that point, the legality of doing so hovered dangerously in the gray area.

Photo courtesy Vic Berg.

Now, fast-forward, and I'm sure you've guessed already. No sooner do we score replacement trophies, pick up the decoys, and load up the boat, then somewhere down-shore Yoda would poke her face out of the edge of the marsh with their bull pintail proudly displayed in her grinning mouth, the other trophy at her feet.

It'd about piss you off how proud of herself she was, but you had to hand it to her — she got me again. Now the gray area was suddenly black and white, but with me on the black side. The worst thing was that I'm pretty sure that this wouldn't be the last time I'd get out-thunk by my brown dog.

Photo courtesy Troy Cranford.

ONLY TWO
FLOCKS

My buddy William has gunned with our guide service for thirty-four of its thirty-five year existence. He and the people he's brought with him have downed better that 500 fowl over the years. William serves as the unofficial historian for Outer Banks Waterfowl, being that he has gunned with nearly every guide and every guide's dog since our inception. As such, he's a good guy to set with a new guide. Through their conversation during the day, the guide cannot help but come away from the hunt with a sense of being a part of the history that has formed in the wake of our service's passage through time.

William seldom ends his day afield skunked. One day I mentioned to William how lucky he seemed to be when he hunted with us.

"What do you mean, lucky?"

"Well, reading your card the other day (I keep a 3 x 5 card for everybody who's ever gunned with us. Among other things, each card lists which guide they hunted with and what they shot each day. William's card is actually eight 3 x 5s stapled one corner to another, so it accordions open when you go to read it. There's writing on both sides of each card), I noticed that you hardly ever get skunked, and you usually do as good or better than anybody else on the days you hunt."

"Luck doesn't have much to do with it," was William's reply.

"Oh. So you're that much better than everybody else?" I teased.

"No. Not so much better as more positively focused," William corrected.

"What?"

"Vic, I'm going to let you in on a little secret," he continued. "It only takes two flocks to have a good day."

He took a tentative sip at the steaming cup of coffee that he'd just poured from his metal thermos. Determining it was too hot to drink, he instead cupped the mug in his hands for the warmth.

"Look at it this way," he went on, "if a flock of a dozen widgeon decoy to us perfectly, it's not out of the question that the three of us could knock out five or seven. Then, in the whole rest of the day, you get only one crack at a bunch of ten mallards. Once again, it's not out of the realm of possibility for us to knock four or six birds out of that bunch."

He let that thought sink in while he tried for another sip at the coffee mug.

"I don't care who you are," he muttered as he finally tasted some coffee, "nine to a dozen big ducks is a good day, and I'm willing to wait for it to happen."

Duck in Sherry Cream Sauce
OVER PUFF PASTRY

If you are lucky enough to go hunting with William, you'll probably come home with some big ducks. For a really gourmet dinner, try this recipe. It's very easy to make and you and your guests will love it!

INGREDIENTS:
1/2 package Pillsbury® Puff pastry
1 cup flour seasoned with salt and pepper
4 duck breasts, deboned and skinned
3 tablespoons butter
1 tablespoon oil
8 mushrooms, cleaned and sliced
3 scallions with greens, chopped
2 cloves garlic, minced
1/4 cup sherry
1 cup cream
1 tablespoon tarragon (2 if fresh)

Cut pastry sheet into 4 rectangles and bake according to directions on package. Turn oven off when they are done. Meanwhile, dredge breasts in flour mixture. Melt butter and oil in large skillet, brown duck breasts on medium high heat. Add mushrooms and scallions and garlic. Cook over medium heat till meat is done to desired tenderness. Remove meat to a platter and cover with foil. Add sherry and cook over high heat for 2-3 minutes, stirring constantly and scraping bottom of pan. Add cream and tarragon to pan, decrease heat to medium and cook till sauce thickens. Add meat to sauce. Split rectangles of pastry down the center, top the bottom piece with meat and then place the top piece of pastry on top of the meat.

ON EXHIBITING BOATING SKILLS

Photo courtesy Vic Berg.

One of the most glorious parts about being a duck guide is the small boat driving. Being that this usually occurs in the worst weather of the year's coldest months, boating concerns make our water fowling endeavors extreme or, in some cases, extremely interesting. Even getting out of a boat can become more interesting than should be the case.

Just because you can look over your boat's edge and see the sound's bottom through the water doesn't mean that your feet will contact said bottom before you run out of boot. There's a surprising amount of energy that nudges one toward a contrary outcome.

Also, when exiting a boat, if your attempt is misjudged, misangled, mistimed, or in any way misguided, it's not hard to "float your hat" and soak your "all the rest." Soaking your "all the rest" in winter is always *not* good. Just when I figure I've exhausted all the ways that one can wet themselves, I seem to come up with another way, and another, and another.

I'd say that, "Never jump out of a boat that isn't tethered, either to pier or to anchor," would be a good rule. I hold this as sacrosanct for my passengers. Small boat operators must, by necessity, also be their own boat handlers. This means that I must regularly eschew my own rule regarding leaping out of perfectly good boats, but somebody's got to do the tethering, boat holding, and anchor setting.

I guess the most important thing I've learned about jumping out of a boat is to never let go of the gunwale with your hands until after your feet have contacted the bottom. Well, maybe that's not the most important thing. Getting both feet out of the boat at the same time should also rate pretty high on any list.

This is one of the reasons why it's so hard to teach life's lessons. When a person strives to share what they've learned concerning a crux point experienced while in the wild, i.e. the need to make sure that both of your feet leave the boat at the same time, listeners find the advice so basic that they often do not contemplate the implications of non-diligence in said matters.

Have you ever stood with one foot on a boat and the other foot on a dock? I've found that you're fine till the boat drifts…well, not far at all, really. Then, a moment; the inevitable becomes the actual. As your legs spread your weight centers and guarantees your demise. You know what's happening but can't do a thing about it.

With your weight centered and your legs spreading, you are powerless to push off in either direction. The only thing you can do is to go down…The first time I ever did this, I was five and my sister, Valerie, was seven. We were on our Grandpa's boat/dock and were fishing for snapper blue fish off the side of the boat. Our minnow trap that held our bait was tied to the dock, so to get more bait I was jumping onto and off the boat and dock. Well, the little snappers got to biting like mad. Things were going nuts. We're both squealing, fighting fish, jumping back and forth, boat to dock and dock to boat.

It's my turn to grab more bait, and I already had two minnows from our killie trap in my hand as I stepped with one foot onto the boat. Right then I remembered that I'd forgotten to put the wooden bait trap back into the water. I turn to correct my oversight…and that's exactly how long it takes for something to go very wrong while on the water, even while tied to a dock.

The really funny thing was that I must have yelled when I realized the situation I was in because Valerie turned just in time to watch my slow-motion dunking. She looked me right in the eye as I did the splits and then kerplunked into the mucky creek.

I must admit, I was relieved when I saw my sister's laughing face looming over me as I arose from under the creek's rank wetness, coughing and spewing. I saw her outstretched hand and, in my young mind, thanked the heavens for our family bond that she would watch over and rescue me. I reached my arm up, expecting to be drug up out of the stinking muck by my loving big sister, only to have her snatch the forgotten minnows from my outstretched hand. And then she went back to fishing. Really! I had to wade the knee-deep, water-covered muck back to shore! The madder I got, the more I fell into the muck. By the time I neared shore, I was rancid; I was a tar baby by the time I got there. I thought Valerie had hurt herself laughing.

Ooh. Ooh! Here's another of my favorite ways to appear simple. I run my boat into shallow water near the blind my party and I are to hunt that day. I turn off the motor and trim it up out of the water. With a bit of a youthful flourish, I stylishly put my palm on my boat's gunwale and, like on a gymnast's pommel horse, swing both legs over the side at once so that I exit the boat in a relatively horizontal position. Man, but it's a stylish dismount.

Now, in mid-air, I catch the toe of my lower boot on the gunwale as my legs fly over the boat's edge. Amazingly, with this set of circumstances, your whole body hits the water at once, face to toes.

Or, how about when you stand on one boat and endeavor to spring lithely onto another boat, dock or whatever? You swing one leg as mightily as you can while pushing off with your rear leg at the same time. Now, add in something slippery and/or wet under your rear push-off leg. In a nanosecond, the swinging leg flies out of the boat at the same instant that the rear, pushing leg falls back into the boat. Your momentum, though, is inexorably forward. I'm sure you can imagine the rest. Long story short, you're in the drink again. It is very difficult to both swim and clutch your crotch…at least in my experience. Any effort expended in trying to retain any dignity is wasted at this point. Don't think there aren't other ways to siphon off dignity when it comes to dismounting boats, either.

Never jump out of a boat on the down-current side. Currents are relentless! (To be honest, jumping off on the up-current side isn't much better as your legs can get swept under the boat. A passenger is way better off waiting for the boat to be anchored so that they can disembark alongside while hanging onto the boat for support.) The bigger the boat, the more tenaciously these suggestions holds true. Once your body gets pushed past perpendicular, you have no leverage, no strength, no hope! You are now soaked and soon to be run over by the boat. There is no effective or graceful exit strategy from here on.

Life sucks in one or two different ways at this point. Either you're being drug, soaked and spitting, over the gunwale of your own boat by your clients or you've got to pull yourself, hand over hand, around to the up-current side of the boat. Down-current is bad because the boat keeps over-running you and pushing you under it. Subsequently, you have no leverage with which you can climb back in.

One day, when I was in Alaska a few years ago, helping to guide a brown bear photo safari, I got to watch somebody else learn this lesson the hard way. I had just jumped out of the boat and was holding it from the up-current side, striving to slow its drift in the swift ten-knot current, when at that critical moment one of the overly confident photographers slid over the down-current transom and almost immediately got pushed past perpendicular by the still drifting boat. I hadn't been able to adequately control the boat's down-river motion yet, and the guy was well into getting run over! I could see he was getting pushed under in veritable slow motion.

In that instant, I had to get my feet under me so that I could spring out of the water high enough so that, while pulling simultaneously with my arms, I could flop most of the way across the boat. Once there, I stretched as far as I could and grabbed…his camera! As I slid back across the boat to my original, up-current position, I thrust the camera and lens into another photographer's arms on the way by. No sooner did my feet hit bottom again than the run-over photographer came up for air on my side of the boat. Quick as a snake, I snagged him and together we stopped the boat and set the anchor.

I half expected to catch hell for not grabbing the guy first, but everybody else aboard that day was experienced enough to know that the inevitable was in motion the second his feet hit the water. From where he disembarked the boat, he was going under no matter what. At that point, the only question was whether the camera and lens were going under also.

From what I had learned while helping the BBC with a snow goose special they were filming a few years prior on location on my marsh in North Carolina, I guessed that the camera and lens were probably worth around twenty-five grand. Came to find out that I was off by ten grand…on the light side!

To a man, including the outfitter who owned the camp where Ellen and I were working that summer's sockeye salmon run, everybody agreed: Grab the camera! Every time!

"If we had to, we could've always gaffed him," offered our outfitter.

"What?"

"We can patch him up for a lot less than the cost of the camera equipment, and he'd have a nifty scar to show off later!"

Yeah. I can see that working.

"Hey baby, want to see where I got gaffed while I was on my Alaskan brown bear photographic safari?"

Hmm. That could work. I was intrigued just writing it down.

Finally, if you are ever, pardon the expression, stupid enough to leave your motor running when you disembark your boat and are standing in the water, you have now put yourself in danger of finding yourself in hugely deep doo-doo. Seriously! Ever see somebody's nose hanging by a flap of skin after being sliced by a boat's prop? I have. I didn't do it, but I saw it. Believe me, the image lingers.

Occasionally, I'll have to start my boat while standing in the water to keep us from being blown back onto a shoal, but I never like it. My advice: Don't ever leave a motor running even if the motor is in neutral. Remember what I said earlier: Currents are relentless! Even in neutral, a boat's prop will spin with the current. It's always spinning, always! Now, factor in that a prop that runs through mud or sand doesn't get dulled, it gets sharpened.

Bad, sharp props. Bad, bad, sharp props!

So raise your right hand and repeat after me: "I will never be outside of a boat whose motor is running."

As your guide, I thank you.

MARSH HEN/ QUEEN OF THE MARSH

Photo courtesy Vic Berg.

A lot of the therapeutic value that one gains during a day afield very often comes as a benefit of visual by-product. Let's be honest. When most people think of hunting and hunters, all they can focus on is the kill. Pulling the trigger…the roar and jolt of your weapon…the finality of your quarry succumbing to your diligence and skill!

Very little of this actually goes on in a typical day's hunt. Most of what goes on is either sitting and waiting, standing and waiting or, for variety, leaning and waiting. The constant here is the waiting; and what you do when you wait, put in the most simple of terms, is look around. It's during your periods of just looking around that most of your fondest memories are etched into your brain.

Of this entire past year's gunning season, one of my most poignant visuals involved a marsh hen — more properly, a Clapper Rail.

I have a blind that qualifies as my safe haven on days of extreme winds and storm. This blind's main function is to be a sanctuary where I can take a party on days that are…how to put it into the proper perspective…hideous.

Hard west winds flood my marsh and, when canted even a little to the south, tend to also coincide with torrential rains. So, knowing that I'll have to deal with at least a few of these types of days every year, I build me an appropriate structure.

It's built on the west bank of an interior creek so that your backs are to the offending winds. It's got a tar-papered roof, slanted to run the rain harmlessly off. Because the days when I use this blind are so extreme that some of my guides can't even get their parties out safely, I've built this rascal big and deep to accommodate extra gunners. It's also tall and, well, just plain comfy in a tempest. I constantly have to fight the urge to hang art on its interior walls.

When the winds are west, nor'west or sou'west, thirty to forty, with gusts over fifty, it's going to pour rain all day and my entire marsh will be flooded a foot underwater, this is the place to be. The flooding doesn't even wet my floor as the blind is erected on a raised platform, above the marsh's muck. To step into the blind, I've set a pair of cinder blocks atop a chunk of plywood to keep them from sinking into the marsh.

It's pouring. I'm gunning by myself. The winds are howling at my back. It's probably around 8:30 and besides the teal I shot at daybreak, I haven't had another shot all morning. I really don't particularly care too much. I'm snug and cozy sitting on a cushion that is nestled on my broad bench, a thermos of hot coffee within easy reach.

The blind's ample roof, combined with the side walls gives my little refuge the feel of a sheltered bus stop, a bus stop with no schedule and no concern of the time spent waiting for a vehicle that will never arrive. No matter, as I travel much further in my wandering mind.

In mid-reverie I espy the little sweet thing. With the wind, the water has been steadily rising since I arrived, predawn, this morning. The top of my cinder block steps is barely underwater. Since I never got around to putting a door on this blind when I built it, I can look out of the opening where the door should have been, and that is where the russet, intricately patterned, beautiful little marsh hen is standing.

She's on top of the cinder blocks with her head cocked to the side. She has a questioning tilt to her demeanor and a shine and clarity expressed through the eye that she is focusing on me. Her message to me, apparent. I am in her house! I can tell that she is calculating whether I can be trusted to share my lee sanctuary.

We must have stared at each other for minutes, ten of them at least. Then she looks over her shoulder and I swear I can see her sigh.

Survival instincts just will not allow her to cross the threshold. Yet, you can sense her reasoning: on the step she is mostly out of the water and the blind is blocking the wind and rain. She'll wait.

She just tucks her long bill under her wing and dozes till I need to leave an hour later. She only flitters off when I leave the blind to get my boat.

After I have all my decoys up and they are stacked meticulously in my boat, I happen to glance through the blind's doorway as I am leaving the creek. There, sitting on the cushion which I left on the bench and out of the rain, is the little marsh hen, very at home in her mansion on the marsh.

I have to laugh at myself and my misguided notions; here I thought I owned the marsh.

DECOY PLACEMENT AND OTHER GOOD STUFF TO KNOW

I'm lucky to hunt water fowl in an area where, on any given day, I can bag any of twenty-five species. Of course, you can't rig representative decoys of all species on any given day. To improve your harvest in general, first and foremost learn to recognize fowl in flight. Secondly, learn the sounds the various species make, and then find the most effective reproducers of those sounds. (Note that I didn't say most expensive.) Learn to work your calls, when to call and, most importantly, when not to call. Why in the world people pick up a call when they spot birds with wings already set toward them is beyond me. How can you possibly improve what is already going on? At most, do a little background "chuckling" with your mallard call.

By far, your greatest asset in water fowling is your decoys. Couple your decoy placement with waterfowl inter-species behavioral tendencies, and you'll guarantee yourself more consistent success.

Where I hunt we shoot mostly puddle ducks. We are also blessed to be surprised at any time by virtually any species of water fowl. This includes geese, swans, sea ducks, mergansers, coots and divers as well as nearly all puddlers. Here's how I rig to assure my best shot at success.

I usually put out a flock of seventy-five to eighty-five decoys. (This is not counting the 50 to 120 snow goose silhouettes that are placed in the Spartina grass behind the blind. We aren't allowed any Canadas, so I don't rig any.) My flock consists of two to fifteen swan (or five brant), six canvasbacks (mostly drakes), thirty widgeon, six to twelve gadwall, two to eight teal (green and/or blue winged), twenty-four to thirty-six pintail, six mallards, two to four blacks, and one to six buffleheads.

My best wind is a side wind, right to left, which for me is from the north. This is the best rig for this situation. Your decoy flock is to be constructed from the farthest point upwind to the farthest point downwind.

I usually employ a modification of a double diamond rig, with an umbrella of swans. Imagine two triangles with their flat bases facing each other and a large, nearly empty space in between. The sharp point of the upwind diamond points directly into the wind. The upwind flock is always the larger of the two. Generally, the larger the decoy, the farther it is placed upwind. The smaller birds won't cross over larger birds when landing. (It's a matter of disrespect to the larger birds, and the smaller will usually receive an ass-whipping and get run off for this transgression.)

In the dark of pre-dawn, everything seems farther away than it really is. Very often, as the sun comes up, you realize that your decoys are way too close to the blind. To combat this (if the water is shallow enough to wade), pace off sixty-five yards from the blind to your farthest decoy upwind, and rig from there. If you can't wade, guesstimate, but your first decoy is the key to work off of.

We hunt wide open areas, so we have to create a flock that can be seen from a long way off. A densely packed flock can be seen from much farther away than a loosely spread flock. I always put some big birds at the very head of the rig in an umbrella shape (either swans, geese or brant) to improve the sight-ability of the rig. They also act to force the ducks to land prior to crossing over them. Start your flock at the extreme edge of shot gun range (sixty-five yards) with your larger birds in an umbrella shape, being beyond shooting range. If you're also hunting the larger birds, they'll be in range on their approach to your decoys.

Swans and your various geese are more adept at feeding than the ducks since their bodies and necks are longer. As such, they have a better reach. Widgeon are natural-born thieves. They steal grass from the larger birds as they come up for air.

Widgeon also thieve from divers. Therefore, the cans are the tip of your upwind diamond, intermingled with the widgeon, and then the gadwalls on the inside.

Gadwalls have an annoying habit of coasting the extreme outer edge of your spread then sitting seventy to seventy-five yards away. They never come closer after landing. That's why your gaddy decoys make up the close point of the upwind flock.

A final finesse point is to make the upwind flock a little asymmetrical. You'll want the close half of the flock to have more birds and be a little larger. Just a smidgen of a hook should grace both the inner and outer edges so the ass end of the flock forms a slight cup. This makes for a nice oval landing zone. The downwind edge should be fifteen to twenty yards to your right as you look straight out (west) from the blind. The outer decoys should be fifty to fifty-five yards from shore.

The downwind flock begins thirty-five to forty yards from the upwind flock's downwind point. It must be tightly packed, symmetrical and closer to shore. It is a lead in to the landing zone. The outside decoy should be thirty yards from shore, and the far downwind decoy should be at the edge of shooting range. The inside point should be five to ten yards from shore.

There can be no pockets or straggling decoys in the outer edges of the downwind flock. If there are, virtually all decoying birds will sit short of your rig, just shy of the pockets or stragglers.

Pintails really dislike crossing over other birds as they land. Blacks refuse to cross over anything. Blacks and mallards hang out together. Therefore, the blacks, mallards, and pintails constitute the downwind flock.

Your black ducks are the most vexing to rig as they sit at the tail of a flock — they won't cross over anything and nothing likes to cross over them. Therefore, I put them on the outside point of the downwind flock, but blended in with the pintails and mallards.

You now have a large empty hole in between the two diamonds. For the finishing touch, put the teal (one to six) in the big empty space. I prefer a group of four teal fifteen yards from shore and another pair a hair farther out and fifteen yards farther upwind.

Your last decoy(s) are the bufflehead. They don't like to hang with any other birds, so set them off by themselves, anywhere, but not within your main rig.

Okay. You're done. Now go stash your boat and shoot some ducks.

Most of your birds will line up on the downwind flock but, since there are no pockets to land in, will coast just to the outside then do a dip and fall in behind the widgeon, just ahead of the teal. Boom! Right where you want them. If they sky rocket with your first shot, the wind will drift them straight over you as they rise.

I love it when a plan comes together.

Photo courtesy Troy Cranford.

A CURMUDGEON'S SET

It's not that I can claim to know all there is to be known about hunting ducks. It's just that I got started at it so early and have been in charge of so many hunting parties over so many years that it just seems that, at this point, I ought to. I've learned to trust my instincts and, hopefully, to recognize what I don't know quickly enough so that I can slow down and figure things out before anybody gets hurt.

When I mention instincts I define them as rote behavior derived at through years of really frightening near misses. I've had hunters decide to test the safety of their loaded shotgun by pulling the trigger in the blind. One blew a hole in the sky, the other the floor. Those could have worked out a whole lot worse. As a group, guides really are not happy when shotguns go off unexpectedly down inside of the blind. The third time this happened to me, the end result was a hole in the blind's wall and the dog nearly shot. New instinct and rule: Never trust anybody whose hand is anywhere near their trigger.

Or, I'm gunning with some guys from Colorado, and they tell me a story about a buddy of theirs whose pal's uncle's best friend had a dog knock a loaded gun off of his cousin's duck blind's seat. As the story was told to me, the gun went off when it hit the floor and blew his partner's arm clean off above the elbow save for a flap of skin that his lower arm swung from.

Now, that's an image that would stick with you. I opt to try and never experience a similar event. New instinct and rule: Never let a dog up on my duck blind's seat. See how this works?

By the time you've hunted multiple decades' worth of entire hunting seasons experiencing many near misses and surviving a few direct hits, it's no wonder that I seem to have rules for everything. Very often I may have forgotten the incident, but the instinct and rule remain...that, in its essence, is how one becomes a curmudgeon.

I've been nearly shot numerous times. I've had pellets rain all around me too many times to count. I've been hit by pellets hard enough to raise blood blisters on my exposed face several times. I've never liked any of these experiences, and each and every one has resulted in a new instinct and subsequent new rule. Like the rule where I always wear a hat with a brim when I dove hunt. I do this not because of any fashion or sun protection sense; rather, it's so I can turn the brim of the hat toward the sound of any nearby gunfire, thereby protecting my eyeballs from getting hit by pellets. I have this thing about not wanting to get shot in the eyeball... either of them.

Here's one of my rules. People who are duck hunting together need to hunt close together. This rule seems to be counter-intuitive. You'd think it would be safer to spread out a little bit. You would be wrong.

Each hunter in a party should never be any farther apart than the length of their shotgun. If any of your group can swing a shouldered shotgun in any direction and end up with a buddy in his/her sights, then he/she/they should move closer together. Everybody should be near enough so that a gun barrel swung carelessly would, at the worst, bounce off of a buddy, but never aim at him.

I've had a swinging gun barrel strike my chest as a gunner was trying to shoot at a duck that had flown around my side of the blind. I was standing and leaning against the blind's rear wall. My hands and forearms were shoved down the tops of my chest waders for warmth. I had been kind of daydreaming and didn't realize that anything was up until the gunner in the middle grabbed his gun. Right about then I saw the drake bufflehead winging around my corner of the blind...then the gun swinging in my direction...I was pinned against the back wall with my hands down my boots and they were hung up on my boot straps so I couldn't free them to swat the gun barrel away...the flat of the gun barrel strikes my chest. The contact of barrel to chest causes the gun's barrel to bounce back off of my chest an inch or so... exactly then...BARROOOOM!

As much as it pissed me off when this occurred, it was still preferable to what would have happened had I been a mere foot farther away! Instead of bouncing off my chest and then firing, loudly but harmlessly in front of me, I'd have had a gaping chest wound where my heart used to be.

As a side note, I didn't say a word after that particular episode. I just went and got the boat and started picking up decoys. Anything I would have said would only have lessened the intensity of what had very nearly just happened. I did not want the knucklehead to forget. I also wasn't sure that I hadn't soiled myself....

At the least, being in the confines of a duck blind helps to keep the gunners hemmed in. By far, the unsafest way to hunt is without a blind and spread out along a shoreline. Hunting without a blind and utilizing natural cover along the shore can be a very effective gunning strategy but only as long as everyone is extremely careful. In particular, decide beforehand whether everyone is going to shoot while sitting or standing. It really does make a difference. You should never do both or someone is liable to lose their head.

Finally, whether in a blind or using natural cover without one, nobody should ever shoot across the group, i.e. the guy on the right doesn't shoot at birds on the left and vice-versa. Even though this is one of my strictest rules, I never trust people to obey it. It doesn't pay to be right when you're shot in the eyeball.

If a bird ever flies low around my corner of the blind and I am gunning with anybody else I never stand up to shoot at it. Rather, I stay seated, put my fingers in my ears and face the other gunners. I never stand up at all because, more times than I care to recall the guy in the middle jumps up and shoots where my head would've been.

This doesn't irk me as much as one might imagine because I half expect it, and I've made sure that I'm already out of harm's way. At this point my main focus is making sure that the guy on the far side of the blind doesn't shoot his buddy in the head, the same buddy who is presently popping a shot off over my head. The next gun barrel that I deflect with my hand immediately prior to the gun going off and potentially killing his buddy won't be the first time I've had to do this. I've also gone to swipe at a barrel and missed...a hair prior to BARROOM! I live with the fear and knowledge that it most likely won't be the last time for either.

Sheesh...careful there, buddy! Consider a gun a light-saber that shoots to infinity. Now, what are you aiming at?

THAT OLD GIFT OF GAB

"Hello?"

"Yes, he is. I'm his wife. Is there anything I can do for you?"

"Questions about a guided hunt? I can answer those for you."

"Um-hmm. Yeah…well, he just walked through the door. He left this morning at 3:45 and it is now 6:55 p.m. He's got to be back to the Sea Ranch in a half an hour to organize tomorrow, and he hasn't eaten yet. He's been in the marsh all day, and it's been blowing a gale since last night."

Photo courtesy Vic Berg.

"How about this? You ask me all of your questions, and if we get to one I can't answer, I'll let you talk to him."

"We try to hunt two to a blind with a guide who stays with you all day."

"No. We don't hunt like that, and, no, we'd never mix you in with another group"

Ellen's voice faded as she headed for the desk in the bedroom where we keep The Book, which is our name for our gunning log.

"January sixteenth and seventeenth? Let me look...."

I was about dozing off when Ellen came back into the living room twenty minutes later. She had a big smile on her face. I'd had one eye on the weather channel and the other eye half shut when she walked in. I focused both wind-wearied, blood-shot eyes onto her big grin.

"What'd you do, eat a canary?"

"What?"

"You look awfully proud of yourself."

"Yeah, well I did just book a group of twelve guys for two days."

"Awesome! Good work. You just made six guides real happy for two more days...what...there's something else. Are you flirting with the clients again?" I asked in mock-disapproval.

"No," she laughed. "But I did get one of the best compliments ever...."

"Okay...."

"After he asked about availability, he wanted to know how we'd been doing, duck-wise. So I told him about the flock of redheads that swarmed Keegan the other day, and how good the swan and teal shooting has been in Currituck, and how Les has been doing on the pintail and redheads and brant on the reef behind Avon, and your shoot in the blizzard yesterday. Then I read him what every guide shot today."

I was chuckling to myself by this time. "Do you think you gave him enough information?" I joked.

"Exactly," she replied. "That's when I got my compliment," Ellen crowed. "He told me that I can talk 'duck' better than any guy that he knows...."

DELILAH'S GRAND ENTRANCE

The life spans of our dogs effectively bracket our own life span. Growing up, it seemed that there was always a Chesapeake Bay retriever dog or two in the house. While technically, they were my Dad's dogs, everyone within the household had to develop their own strategies for dealing with the big headstrong chuckleheads.

Photo courtesy Troy Cranford.

Abbey was our first Chessy. I believe that we got her when I was four or five. She was one of those awesome dogs — copasetic in the house and relentless afield. I don't recall that she ever bit me. She lived a good and full life up to the point when my Dad accidentally shot and killed her while they were gunning out of his boat one day. She jumped up on the seat just as the gun went off. I don't ever recall my Dad being more pensive or remorseful, as they had been intensely close as gunning buddies. Her accidental death stung him bad. I'm sure it's why I was drilled on safety measures as strongly as I was as we grew up hunting together. In my Dad's mind, it could have just as easily been him or me floating, unresponsive, with the outgoing tide.

Delilah was Vern's replacement dog. She had belonged to an older gentleman who had recently passed away. The previous owner had been strictly old school in regard to Delilah and had never allowed her house pet status. For the first two and a half years of her life, she was only allowed out of her pen to either train or to hunt. She had never even seen the inside of a human abode until the day my Dad went and got her. Unsocialized to humans at all, she was, to a kid's eye, delightfully whacky.

I still remember when we first got Delilah. It wasn't long after the hunting accident that my Dad heard of the widow with the trained Chessy who couldn't give the dog the attention that it needed. It only took one meeting between the widow and the uniformed Navy Chaplain to arrange a week-long hunt for himself and Delilah on North Carolina's remote Outer Banks. If the dog hunted, she had a new home.

Back then, my Dad had befriended a young heathen Outer Banker named Jimmy Curling, whose family owned a small motel cottage court called the Buccaneer Motel. In trade for help with building duck blinds and fill-in guiding, Jimmy gave my Dad his own motel unit for each entire duck season. In true bachelor fashion (I can't remember a female, or anyone else prone to spontaneous straightening up, ever having a reason to enter our "hunt camp"), our motel unit was a mess with all manner of hunting paraphernalia by mid-season. A pile of newly repaired decoys were here, duck calls over there, ammo boxes, dishes on the table and in the sink, ever present coffee maker on the counter, pots and pans on the stove, boots and clothes drying by the heater, a shotgun dismantled and in pieces atop the dresser awaiting cleaning and repair, more cased guns leaning against the chair. In short, any flat surface was occupied with guy stuff.

I remember showing up at the Buccaneer with Delilah in her crate in the back of our old VW bus on a clear December morning. As we pulled up, Jimmy was waiting for us in the motel's parking lot. Vern had called ahead and told him about the new dog — a field champion — and Jimmy was eager to meet her.

When Delilah first sprang from her crate, we could all tell that she was skittish and hadn't been socialized with humans, but she obeyed her commands and she behaved well when on her leash. My Dad threw a retrieving dummy a few times and we all agreed that, yes sir, she sure looked like a fine Chesapeake Bay retriever dog.

About this time, Vern presented Jimmy with a bottle of top shelf, really expensive, seven-star…some kind of liquor that he'd brought back from his last Naval deployment to the Mediterranean Sea or from a Caribbean cruise, I don't remember which. I remember my Dad was real proud of these bottles of liquor and had even let me touch the seven stars that were embossed along the top of the bottles' label.

I guess my Dad was expecting that Jimmy would save and cherish the gift until some evening in the future, after they'd just shared the hunt of a lifetime and were anointing the memory thereof with Vern's freshly opened, seven-star elixir that had been painstakingly transported halfway around the world.

Yeah, not so much of that.

Instead, Jimmy immediately opened the bottle and poured a generous dollop into his half-finished mug of over-percolated, lukewarm coffee. He took a good pull at the mug then smacked his lips appreciatively a few times.

"Dag, that must be real good liquor. It's so smooth…you can't even taste it over the coffee."

I actually thought my Dad might cry, the way that his expectations were being desecrated. Jimmy had never even looked at the seven stars that the liquor bottle so proudly displayed on its front. I watched my Dad's mouth open and shut, but he couldn't think quick enough to know how to respond. Before he could utter a word however, Jimmy poured an equally generous dollop into my Dad's ever present coffee mug.

"Tell me, can you even taste the liquor? Mmm, smooth," Jimmy purred.

I remember watching my Dad staring deeply into the very bottom of that mug. I could almost see his grand illusions evaporating with the steam from the coffee. He sighed.

"If you can't beat 'em… " I heard him mutter as he downed a gulp of his own.

At this point it's important to recall that these were simpler days. Despite being in my early teens, I was pretty much an innocent. My Dad took his occupation as a man

of the cloth and role model seriously, so we kids had been way shielded growing up. I had never seen alcohol in action. This day was taking on an edginess that fairly burst with energy. I knew that I would not be allowed to participate in the grown-up stuff, but I was sure as heck going to pay attention on this day. You could just tell that things were on the verge of getting nutty.

Jimmy had already finished his cup of "coffee," and Vern wasn't far behind. As Jimmy ducked into his own cottage for a fresh spot of coffee, my Dad had me hold the dog while he went about hiding some cloth-bound boat fenders that we were using as retriever dummies. We wanted to see if Delilah could cipher out some blind retrieves.

The dog did great, and with each sip of coffee the men seemed to get more and more enthusiastic about the new dog's prowess. Several blind retrieves and another cup of "coffee" later and the guys are getting into the blind retrieves. They took turns. One would hold the dog as the other would go about hiding the three dummies all about the grounds of the cottage court.

With each dummy retrieved, the energy level and revelry increased. Soon, we're all cheering and shouting encouragement. Each time, the next guy gets to hide the dummies, and with every subsequent turn they get more creative in their attempts to stump the retriever dog. The boat fenders get stashed behind trash cans, under decks, on car tires, in patches of weeds and under upturned boats. The dog finds them all. Soon, Vern and Jimmy are running all over acting more like kids than kids. I'm so caught up in the madness by this time that I've been reduced to spinning in circles and laughing.

Suddenly, we all get serious again. It seems the bottle of seven star elixir is empty and Vern has let it slip that he has one more bottle stashed in his bag in our cottage. Like lightning after a metal object, Jimmy's off, heading for the other bottle, coffee mug in hand despite Vern's suggestion that, "Maybe, like. You know. Maybe we'd like to save that bottle for later."

"Nah," Jimmy threw over his shoulder as he headed for our cottage, "later always takes too long getting here and when it does get here, it's never soon enough. Besides, we might as well ride this bull while we got him between our legs…at least, that's what I like to tell the ladies," Jimmy added with a wink.

It was pretty evident to Dad and me that if we didn't want our cottage ransacked, we'd best produce the other bottle. We headed for our cottage, dog in tow.

When we all got there, Jimmy had already pushed through the screen door and, as his eyes adjusted to the dimness inside, commented on all the stuff that we'd accumulated in half of a season's worth of fowling.

"What'd you do, buy 'Orvis'?" he asked, surveying all our cammo stuff arrayed on every surface in the room.

My Dad had stopped at the threshold of our cottage with the dog at heel. I was following behind them. My Dad asked no one in particular, "I wonder if I should bring her into the cottage. She's never been in a house before." Just then we both looked through the screen door as Jimmy upturned a suitcase onto a bed.

"I guess she'll have to learn sometime," under his breath, and louder, "Whoa there, Hoss, the bottle's over there on the table in one of the food boxes. I'll get it." As he hurried across the room, he unsnapped Delilah's leash along the way.

Maybe it was the screen door slamming behind me as I entered the room, or maybe it was the shock of the volume of human scent and all our stuff that the dog had never experienced before. Either were probably contributing factors, but I still to this day believe that the lunacy and drunk of the day had somehow got into the dog because, unbeknownst to the two of them who were discussing whether to have one more drink from the new bottle in Vern's hand or finish off that bottle also, the dog in one instant reverted to her inner beast.

Evidently, a cur's inner beast feels safest at increased levels of altitude. In the instant that the screen door slammed, several things occurred in unison. The men quit quibbling and turned toward the sound of the slamming door just as the dog decided to get to a higher vantage point to better survey her outlandish surroundings. And in that instant, she sprang.

The first thing that she landed on was the nearest bed that had the suitcase dumped onto it. Throw a hundred pounds of dog on any bed and inanimate stuff is going to do what inanimate stuff does in that instance. It flew up in the air and landed on the floor with a crash. That startled the dog so much that she jumped onto the night stand. The lamp and alarm clock hit the floor at about the same time. Somehow, that set off the clock's alarm, which startled the dog even more.

Already accustomed to the bounce of the bed from her first leap, she used the extra impetus from landing on the second bed to launch herself across the room and onto the dining table, flying right between Jimmy and Vern, who were too shocked to move. Three boxes of groceries and glassware hit the floor. CRASH-INKLE-inkle-inkle! The table tilted and the dog had no option but to jump again, this time landing, splayed and sliding, along the length of the breakfast bar. All that stuff hit the floor.

Just then, Jimmy let out a war-whoop and guffawed so hard that he farted. He spun in mock horror at his own flatulence and bumped the teetering table enough to send it crashing toward the floor also, which lands atop and scattered the pile of repaired decoys. Vern made a belated grab at the dog that had already flown past him, spilled the table, slid along the breakfast bar, and, before falling off of that, was now in mid-air and headed for the kitchen's counter that hems in the back wall and sink that are, unfortunately, cluttered with about all of our dirty pots and pans at the present moment.

I figure she wasn't expecting the slipperiness of the countertops because she hit that surface scrabbling all four legs at once, so besides sending all the pots and pans clattering in all directions, she actually sped up her momentum, which propelled her across the stove top, where the pots and pans were even dirtier, and hit the floor with vigor nonetheless.

Jimmy's laughter is beyond hysterical at this point, and I'm not sure that he hasn't blown boogers out his nose from laughing so hard. He's bent over at the waist with his hands on his knees as the dog continues her circuit of the interior of our cottage. She gains her momentum against the back wall and leaps again; this time she's headed for the chair that all the cased shotguns were leaning against. Of course, it and they couldn't contain that level of momentum and, as the guns scattered and the chair toppled, Delilah took her final leap onto the only surface in the room yet unscathed.

She hit the top of the dresser with her front legs, but not her back ones. The dismantled shotgun literally flew in every direction as the dog clung to the dresser's edge with her elbows while her rear legs scrabbled up the dresser's side. The case of ten boxes of twenty-five shotgun shells apiece was the last thing to fall from atop the dresser. Of course, all ten boxes spewed their contents when they hit the floor and the shells rolled quietly as a silent tribute to the powers of inner beast and momentum. The clock's alarm continued to blare.

Achieving her balance and reigning in her momentum atop the dresser, Delilah had finally achieved the elevation and position that her inner beast demanded. Satisfied, she sat and looked about innocently. I swear she yawned.

This brought about another war-whoop from Jimmy and another fart. Once again he spun around in mock horror at his own flatulence. In the process, he stepped on several rolling shotgun shells, lost his balance, and fell onto the bed. He hit the bed at an odd angle and bounced off and fell onto the floor. He lay there on his side guffawing and trying to wipe the boogers from his nose with his sleeved arm.

And Vern? I stood in the doorway and watched as, in his present state, he reacted about two counts behind the brown blur that encircled our little cottage that morning, focusing from point of chaos to point of chaos, until he was left staring at the taciturn Chesapeake Bay retriever dog sitting stoically atop the dresser...at which point he fell to the ground laughing like I'd never seen a preacher laugh before or since.

Me? I vowed right then and there that there were two certainties in life. One, that I would never miss going on one of these trips; and, two, that when I got older, I was going to have me one of these crazy brown beasts.

And people think that hunting is just about the killing.

VERN'S LOGS LOST

After looking everywhere I could think to look, I finally had to admit that my Dad's duck hunting log books were gone! I'd asked my mom, Vera, if she'd seen them, and after looking around on her own she had reported that she must have thrown them out when she cleared out some of Vern's seminary notes and books. He'd been gone five years; it was time for that chore.

Photo courtesy Troy Cranford.

My heart absolutely sank when she'd said that, though.

"Threw them out?!" I didn't actually say it the way I thought it. In my mind I screamed it with fervor. Out of my mouth it was more like, "You looked everywhere? Maybe they're at my place. I'm pretty sure I left them at your house though, because my house is more susceptible to the hurricanes."

I was pretty nonchalant about it because if they were gone, then there was nothing else for it. They were just gone. There was no reason to make my Mom feel worse.

But I was devastated! My heart sank as bad as when my first true love told me that we no longer were…and wouldn't be again! How crushed can one be? At least with the puppy love I learned that with time the pain does yield and, lo-and-behold, you eventually find new love, but Vern's gunning logs were another matter entirely! They could not be replaced. They were a visceral connection, one of the few that I had left.

From the very first day that Vernon E. Berg, Junior, who was born and raised on Long Island, just outside of New York City, first pulled on warm clothes and heavy rubber boots, took up a scatter-gun, and explored varied waters in search of wary wild fowl, he had kept meticulous records of every day he'd spent afield.

Every day, every gunning buddy, every duck, goose, grebe or cormorant felled in his lifetime was recorded in those logs. He also faithfully recorded the locations, the dates gunned, the time, the weather, the tides and his gunning buddy's kill totals. And, finally, and my personal favorite, he had a column for every day headed Remarks. It is amazing how a few words from so long ago can put you back into that same day again…gunning with my Dad.

In the Remarks column were his observations of that day in particular: the cool things that were seen, the birds that were missed, just the feel of the day. Heck, he even drew a map of almost every area that he gunned; he included land and water, wind direction and where he placed each of his duck, goose and/or brant decoys. And now, twenty-five years' worth of all of this was gone! Gone! Gone! Gone!

But, like the pain from the loss of your adolescent love, eventually you regroup and move on. I still had all of my own logs, but they weren't Vern's, and they didn't cover all of those early years. I really had lost a connection.

A year passed as did another half year…another gunning season as well. Ellen, our dogs, and I were doing our best to withstand another typically miserable February on the Outer Banks. Then, on a quintessentially hideous winter's eve, our phone rang. No. Not a cell phone. This was back in the day when you actually had to get up and go to the wall to answer the phone. You didn't even know who was on the other end until after you picked it up.

"Hello?" into my end.

"Vern in New York" by Copy Berg.
Courtesy of Valerie J. Berg Rice.

On the other end I heard: "Hey, Vic. It's Mom. No, I'm good. Look, I found these notebooks you were looking for a couple years ago. No, really. They were in a box that was shoved under some other stuff in the corner of the garage. No, they look to be in good shape. Do you want to just pick them up when you come over for dinner on Sunday? What? Right now? Are you sure? You know how awful it is outside, right? Okay, see you in a bit. And, Vic…Vic? Oh, I guess he hung up already…."

I've never let them out of my house since.

Vern's First and Last

Vern's first day gunning was on October 24, 1959, along the banks of the Delaware River. Only geese were in season with ducks becoming legal in mid-November. He hunted alone in a drizzle until he had to quit for the day at 9 a.m. He never raised his gun or fired a shot all morning.

Two days later, Vern rowed from his father's summer house in Mastic Beach on Long Island, New York, across the sound to the back side of Fire Island-Patter-nack (*sic*) Little Inlet. He sat in a drizzling rain and with a light southerly breeze from 3 p.m. till dark. He passed on many close shots at yet to be legal ducks and settled for a nice pair of brant, his first-ever fowl. On November 17th, when ducks became legal, Vern scored his first duck ever, a black duck taken while gunning out of Mastic Beach again. This time he was opposite from the Forge River.

Twenty-five years later, Vern shot his last duck. It was a drake pintail harvested from our marsh in the Oregon Inlet area of North Carolina.

In between Vern's first and last ducks, a little better than 3.000 other fowl also were felled by the gunning Reverend.

Vern's Fowling, By the Numbers

By the end of the '81/82 waterfowl season, the third to last season of a twenty-five year fascination with gunning waterfowl, Vern did his last big tally. The log book shows that he had harvested 2,929 birds. Of this total there were thirty-four species, thirty-seven if you count grebes, cormorants or a loon. Vern counted everything.

The cormorant and loon were honest mistakes, but the fourteen grebes met their demise on painfully slow days as training aids for our retriever dogs.

I understand that some may not appreciate the raw data, but I'm crazy for totals like these. The following is a listing of fowl that make up Vern's nearly 3,000 bird total.

Vern never was much of a goose hunting specialist. He'd harvest geese, but they were usually a by-product of his duck hunting. I remember a day in the early 1970s that best illustrates his preference for ducks.

We were having one of the best brant (a smallish goose) hunts of my entire life on a before-school hunt in the Lynnhaven Bay area of Virginia Beach, Virginia. We had already harvested a small pile of brant and had just risen to fire into yet another flock of thirty to fifty birds when I noticed, out of the corner of my eye, my Dad shooting at odd angles relative to the flock of decoying geese. It seems he was picking out the occasional widgeon that were intermingled with all the decoying geese. Me? I never even noticed that there were any ducks mixed among all the swirling, cackling brant.

In his accounting at the close of the 1982 season, Vern had harvested thirty-nine Canada geese, fifty-three greater snow geese, and forty-two brant. On the odd list he added four lesser snow geese with one of those being a blue goose. He also shot a single lesser Canada goose.

Puddle ducks are to most fowlers the elite division of water fowling due to the increased levels of wariness these tip-feeders display in the process of decoying. It also doesn't hurt that they are arguably the most consistently palatable, and certainly the more stridently colored, of the various waterfowl divisions. Vern had a good handle on the nuances of decoying and harvesting these most prized of fowl.

The following listed in the order of most harvested to least: black ducks–215, mallards–200, pintail–187, widgeon–136, gadwall–129, green winged teal–121, wood ducks–31, shovellers–31, blue winged teal–10, European widgeon–2.

Diver ducks refers to the class of waterfowl that include the duck population's best swimmers. Their legs are placed further to the rear of their bodies, which gives their webbed feet much more thrust per kick while underwater.

For the most part, this group of fowl is colored only in splashes of black and white and are much drabber than the brilliantly hued puddlers. Divers also tend to be gamier on the table. None of this bothered Vern. He was no elitist. Divers decoy much more easily than the puddlers. Bring 'em on!

The following are listed in decreasing order of fowl harvested: buffleheads–258, American goldeneye–130, greater scaup–129, ruddy ducks–120, lesser scaup–68, canvas back–60, redheads–40, ring necks–26, Barrow's goldeneye–4.

Sea ducks refer to the most extreme of the diver ducks. They are rarely encountered nearer than a half-mile from land. They are all mostly gnarly/gamey, palate-wise.

The following are Vern's sea duck totals: old squaw–35, surf scoters–15, American black scoters–13, white winged scoters–13, American eider–5.

This accounting would not be complete without the merganser/miscellaneous division. This division includes the fowl that most consider most foul! We ate them all though. The lowly coot could be the most under-appreciated of all the fowl. Most gunners mistakenly assume the coot tastes as bad as its appearance is unattractive. They'd only be kind of right.

Just shot, cleaned, cooked and eaten, the coot is poor fare as assumed. The "ass-of-u-and-me" in this situation is buttermilk. When freshly cleaned, coot soaked overnight in buttermilk become delectable. Even their legs are delicious, especially in a rich gumbo. Vern was a believer!

Here is the accounting of Vern's miscellaneous waterfowl: coot–515(!), red-breasted merganser–143, (of anything in our upbringing, the eating of this many mergansers would approach the closest us kids ever came to being abused. I'm just kidding. It is possible to render mergansers tolerable… no, really!), hooded mergansers–48, grebe–14, American mergansers–5, cormorants–4, loon–1, purple gallinule–1.

November 10, 1960

Blind number eighteen: The first time Vern hunts waterfowl on the Outer Banks of North Carolina. he downs two Canada geese with one shot while his gunning buddy is hiking back to the car for the cigarettes he forgot to pack when he set out in the morning. A legacy is set in motion — the remote sand-banks get in your bloodstream and never let you go!

Photo courtesy Troy Cranford.

The Good Old Days

During Vern's second full waterfowl season in 1960, he was lucky enough to hunt waterfowl on thirty-seven occasions. On twenty-two of those hunts, he ended the day totally skunked! I believe I come about my patience honestly. Enduring twenty-two skunk days in one season and not quitting to try something else is a fairly decisive indicator of a man's passion and perseverance. It also just goes to show that there are skills involved that need to become ingrained.

No Mas

In Vernon's entire water fowling career, he crushed the most ducks when he was stationed at the Great Lakes training center in Illinois. The U.S. Naval facility is located on the southern edge of Lake Michigan.

Along a half-mile stretch of the lakeshore, the Navy created a harbor for small boats. The harbor itself was created/rimmed by a nearly continuous (except for the harbor mouth) breakwater that stood above the water maybe eight or ten feet. The continuous walls of the jetty were not much wider than an arms-width, as I recall. Large boulders had been piled loosely along the breakwater's outer edge to help absorb the energy of the oft-pounding waves.

Imagine in your mind's eye that you are viewing the harbor from a sea gull's perspective, a thousand feet up in the sky. The harbor would appear to be a white, froth-skirted, rectangle-shaped, calmness along the Great Lakes' shoreline. There was an open mouth, a span of some fifty yards, that

spat out into the depths of the huge lake from the center of the most seaward wall.

One day Vern noticed a nuance of the little harbor. Depending on the wind's slant relative to the shoreline, a natural lee would be created along the wall of the harbor, perpendicular to the shore, that was the most downwind. As a bonus, the fowl had learned to feed on the environment that had evolved within the jetty's loosely piled boulders. One final bonus was how well Vern's pumpkin seed layout boat resembled the loosely piled boulders.

Hunting almost entirely by himself one season, mostly on either downwind lee of the little harbor, Vern harvested better than three hundred fowl. As I recall, he mostly shot greater and lesser blue bills, golden eyes, old squaws, and mallards.

It was 1979 and I was in college at Lake Forest. I was determined to get the most out of that situation, so I had been declining Vern's invitations to share in his fowling bonanza. Finally, toward the end of the gunning season, I relented. What I didn't take into account was how cold it had gotten.

We agreed to hunt the next morning and showed up at the harbor's boat house before dawn. Vern was the only person loony enough to be on the big lake this time of year, so the harbor master had given him his own key to the boathouse. It was a neat, old, stone boathouse that sported a false floor and a hoist to raise and lower his boat into or out of the water.

As Vern went about readying and lowering his boat into the water under the boathouse, he told me to drive around to the lee foot of the harbor's rim while he motored the boat out of the harbor mouth and around to where I was going to be. Then, he was going to set his decoys along that lee leg about two hundred yards out from the shore. Once that was done, he was going to anchor his boat among the rocks and hunt until he had to go retrieve a bird or birds. Then I'd swap places and hunt till I had to retrieve fowl, and so on.

What this plan didn't take into account was how freaking cold it had gotten. Overnight, the weather had plunged to its heartless, Yankee-cold, bitter, winter worst. The temperature had barely broken above freezing for the last week and a half, so I thought I was ready for frigidity. It hadn't really registered with me when Vern had joked about a Lake this Great being too mean-spirited to freeze.

As I parked the car at the foot of the downwind leg of the harbor wall, I turned off the engine and admired the pre-dawn blush of morning shimmering on the surface of Lake Michigan.

I sat and waited as I tried to spy the boat's running lights leaving the harbor mouth. I got antsy. I opened the door to go pee…I slammed it shut again!

Ow! It's cold! It felt like it must be, like, two degrees out there! I still had to go, probably even more now…braced for the cold…aagh!

By the time I'm done, I can barely feel my fingers enough to zip up. No kidding!

This close to the water in the Great White North in the middle of winter is a brutal zone on the outskirts of Hell. I dive back into the car and restart the engine, although this is made difficult by the fact that my fingers really had quit working due to the cold and I had to grip the car's key with the heels of my hands when I needed to twist it to make the engine catch and roar to life. I revved the engine to rewarm the motor and cranked the heater and fan to their most wide open settings.

As my grandfather used to say, "Holey jump up and sit down, it's cold out there!" I'm pretty sure I saw my pee hit the ground and bounce like little golden BBs.

I rummaged around in the car and endeavored to put on every item of winter clothing that I could find. I sat in the car with the doors closed and the engine and heater on. I worried about carbon monoxide and how long it might take to asphyxiate. (I can't be exactly positive that the car needs to be in a garage for you to die or does the poison gas just seep in through the floor.)

I turn the car back off. I sit in the center of the huge clothing bundle that I have constructed around myself on the front seat of the closed-up car. I idly watch the boat's lights glide into view and stop a couple hundred yards out from where I was. I watched the lights glide about as Vern set his decoys out in the shimmering near darkness.

I marvel that his clothes must be the best and warmest that money can buy to be out in his boat in that bitterness. I try to bolster myself with bravado and assure myself that if the old guy could do it, I could do it too.

As I'm having these thoughts, the boat's lights seem to be growing more and more opaque. I surmise that the problem must be caused by my contact lenses. I squeeze shut and reopen my eyes. I stare as hard as I can and try to control the very apertures of my irises. This doesn't work.

Then it dawned on me that the lights had become diffused because of the ice patterns that had formed on the inside of the car's windows from the moisture in my breath. In my mind, this endeavor was beginning to border on stupid. It's a wise man who won't be sucked into stupid. Apparently, I wasn't that guy.

I've hiked to the crest of the Continental Divide in Colorado and skied, out of bounds, the miles to the highway down below. I was at altitude, well above the tree line, and that cold didn't even compare to this cold. This cold sucked! Sorry. There's no other word for it. This cold just sucked, bad! I reminded myself to borrow my Dad's boots and gloves when it was my turn. I tried again with the bolstering…it couldn't get but so bad as long as I could keep my fingers and toes warm. Yeah….

Before long, the day began to brighten. Not long after that, I heard three, evenly spaced shots rumble across the water. They served to startle me back to my frozen misery. The cold had gotten into my head and was playing games with my brain. I had given up worrying about asphyxiation and had shifted my focus to trying to physically absorb and store every degree of heat that was coming out of the car's floor vents as the motor hummed in the background.

Suddenly, the passenger side door opened and Vern tumbled in. As he slammed the door, he began slapping his thighs with his gloved hands to better facilitate blood flow to his legs and hands.

"Holy crap, but it's cold out there!" he roared as he slap-slapped his thighs. He cursed more than any of his other preacher friends that I'd been around. I called him on it once. He assured me that the Catholic priests swore way more than he did. I had no reason to doubt him and, being how in my mind he spoke for God, I didn't.

"What'd you get?" I asked, in the hope that focusing on the hunt would fire my juices and better inure me to the cold.

"A pair of drake goldeneyes. Hey, did I tell you I got a pair of Barrow's goldeneyes last week? Counting those two, that makes three for my whole life," he answered, all the while slap-slapping his thighs. "I tried for the triple, but the last bird wouldn't fall. Pellets hit all around that last bird," he continued. "Tough, tough, birds! Did you know, I've shot so many ducks this year that I don't even sit up to shoot unless I feel like I can get two birds crossing, with one shot, or a three-shot triple…especially with the divers and sea ducks."

He paused a minute as he pulled off his gloves and shook his fingers hard, repeatedly, by snapping his wrists. "It's just cold as blazes out there," he marveled. "Okay, okay, I admit it," Vern confessed without any prodding. "I never pass on puddlers. I only do that finicky stuff with the divers," he went on. "Your mother and I have eaten about all the sea ducks we can stand, but danged if they don't fly so pretty that it's hard not to pull the trigger…you'll see. Have a go. It's your turn," he encouraged as he motioned me toward the door.

"Here," he offered, "borrow my gloves and boots. You're going to need them." He thrust his gloves into my arms and kicked his boots over to me after sliding them off of his feet. "Is your hat warm enough? Okay…have at 'em," he left hanging in the air as he pushed me out the door and into the bitter cold.

I quickly grabbed my old Browning, auto-five and a couple fistfuls of shells from the car's trunk. I shoved the shells into my pants pockets as I headed out along the top of the harbor wall the 200 yards to where Vern had left the little layout boat hooked to the seawall.

When I got within about fifty yards of the boat, a trio of old squaw got up from the far side of the decoy rig and winged out toward the open lake. I didn't take a shot because I didn't want to wound a sea duck with a long shot and have to chase it all over heck and back. I was real careful getting into the boat. I did not want to fall in today. I'd be frost-bit before I could get back to the car, assuming I didn't drown.

As I eased in, I climbed under the boat's camouflaged canvas cover. I lay down in the boat and adjusted the backrest so that my eyes were the only thing peeking out from under the canvas, like crocodile eyes in a still pond. I laid my now loaded gun, quartered across my chest, atop the canvas and pointed to the left of my feet and down-range, ready to grab in an instant if need be.

Then I proceeded to wait. The little dose of warmth that I had generated walking to the boat was gone in the first five minutes. I waited some more. The cold returned with a vengeance.

One of the drawbacks to gunning from a layout boat is that they are heat vampires. Being that a boat's hull is only so thick, and the water under the boat is so very cold, the cold of the water trumps your body's ability to generate heat and every erg of heat is drawn out through the very skin of the boat. I was freezing! I was way ready to shoot something just so my turn in the boat would be over, but nothing wanted to come near me. I waited some more. Even seagulls weren't flying.

And then the dreaded layout boat-butt started. Boat-butt is a legitimate phenomenon. Something about lying on the floor of a cold boat combined with your extra layers of clothes makes your butt itch like fire. I had forgotten what a torture device a layout boat could be…and still, nothing moving.

Thankfully, my Dad's boots and gloves were doing their jobs and my toes and fingers weren't hurting but so bad. It's just that I was starting to get cold in my body's core. This kind of cold starts at your coccyx and slowly crawls up your spine. This is the same cold that lets you know it's time to quit when you're wet-suited and winter surfing in frigid waters.

Right then, I remembered that my Dad's metal Stanley thermos was somewhere in the bottom of the boat. I knew from past experience that any thermos of Vern's would have hot coffee in it. I rummaged around till I found it down around my feet. I worked it with my feet up to where I could reach it with my hand.

The thermos of hot coffee fueled my optimism. I really didn't want to be a wuss and quit before my turn was over. Maybe a dollop of steaming brew could help keep me in the boat a few more minutes.

And then I saw them. My salvation! A bunch of a dozen or so blue bills were in the air. They'd just come into view as they cleared the most seaward elbow of the marina wall.

Immediately, they spotted my decoys and wheeled toward my clandestine hidey-spot. Quickly, I assessed my situation.

Usually, I'd pass on the blue bills because of their strong and somewhat offensive taste, but they represented to me my ticket out of this slice of winter hell. At this point, I'd eat 'em raw on the spot if that's what it took to get me out of this torture device referred to as a layout boat.

I hate shooting while wearing winter gloves. They're really too cumbersome for the job. You run the risk of accidentally discharging your weapon when you go to get your shooting finger into your trigger guard. And then, you have little sense of the pressure necessary to apply to the trigger itself to make the gun go off.

I'd already put the thermos down. My hands were under the boat canvas, so I quickly tugged off both my gloves. Then, while never taking my eyes off of the approaching flock but still feeling for my gun, every bird in the bunch quit flapping and locked their wings out. They were in a sixty mile an hour power tumble into the open hole Vern had left in the center of the decoy spread.

Remember a second ago when I said "… while never taking my eyes off of the approaching flock?" Well, I probably should have, but then I really had no experience with this degree of cold to have known to forewarn myself.

As the free-wheeling flock of fowl was making their final approach, my right, ungloved hand had wormed its way above the canvas and was feeling around, blindly, for my gun. After what seemed like an eternity of fumbling around as the birds blew into the rig, the knuckle of my first finger contacted the gun's metal barrel. I shifted my grip to get the gun in my palm as I planned to sit up, firing. That never happened.

When I shifted my grip, I felt a little pull and a sting where my knuckle had touched the gun. It was then that I noticed my hand didn't slide at all after it touched the gun's barrel — and where my hand was gripping the gun barrel ached and burned in a weird way.

I tried to drop the gun to relieve the burn…I couldn't. Ow! I shook my hand…worse. OW! OW!

Oh, my…my hand is frozen to my gun! What do I do?! I'm stuck to my gun like a double dog dare tongue to a lamppost. What do I do? I've forgotten all about the ducks, which are now flaring like a flurry of bottle rockets from the boulder that just yelped and sat up. What do I do? Ow! Ow! Ow!

Coffee! The idea flashed into my brain like the Word of God. Coffee on hand…I'd knocked the canvas back when I sat up. I noticed that, true to form for blue bills, the flock had regrouped and were once again heading into the decoys. I was pretty well occupied with other stuff to pay them much mind. I saw the thermos on the floor of the boat. With my ungloved left hand, I snatched at the thermos' metal screw cap that also served as the cup and swung the body of the thermos under my right arm to provide leverage so I could unscrew and free the cup.

Because of the burning in the palm of my right hand and the open trickle of blood where I'd pulled off a patch of skin from when my knuckle first touched the gun's barrel, I never even noticed the weird tingle on the skin of the fingers that gripped the cup…until I twisted the cup to unscrew it from the thermos.

Actually, that part of the plan worked to perfection…it's just that when I opened my fingers to get another grip on the cup to give it another twist, I instead tightened the cup back onto the thermos.

"What?" I looked at the thermos like it was somehow defective. I tried again to unscrew the cap. Then, instead of further loosening, I snugged the cup back to the thermos. "What, the…."

Right then the weird tingle where my fingers touched the cup ignited into burning pain! "What the…." I tried to drop the thermos…I couldn't. "Wha…oh, oh!" Oh my God! My hand is frozen to the stupid cup, too!

For a moment, it flashed through my brain that this may be how my Dad would find my body — a near-perfect image of a fowler, frozen in his boat with a thermos frozen to one hand and his trusted fowling gun frozen to the other, ducks swimming in the decoys.

"That's it! No mas!"

RETIREMENT?

About a decade ago, I swore to myself that I'd about had it with guiding, and I meant it. I told Ellen of my change of heart. I expressed myself eloquently and with firm resolve. I'd had it. Enough, with catering to others' needs! I was going to shoot me some birds on my own and see what my marsh could do with me and my murderous bastard buddies gunning with menace and abandon.

Photo courtesy Vic Berg.

"Just think how many birds we could shoot if we got in there in the morning, shot what came to us then got out of there and let the marsh alone the rest of the day. Man, it's going to be bee-yoo-ti-ful!" I enthused to Ellen.

Her response: "Um, Vic…you know that if you're not guiding, you don't get to hunt every day, don't you?"

"What?!"

"You can hunt on your days off and maybe some after you get off work, but you're going to have to get another job."

"Oh."

Needless to say, I'm still guiding as hard as I can guide!

Photo courtesy Vic Berg.

The Secret to my Success

I possess a knack that sets me apart from most others, a skill-set, really: I can sit and do nothing better than most anybody.

I'm serious!

If doing nothing were a sport, I'd hold the Olympic and world titles! And, I'm not just a fair-weather-nothing-doer. I can do nothing in truly extreme conditions and for mind-numbingly long blocks of time.

Sure, most folks are probably thinking to themselves that a knack for doing nothing isn't much of an accomplishment to hang your hat on. To that, my response would be that an unfair assumption has probably been made.

Just because the task that I've set my mind to accomplishing will most likely involve a good portion of sitting around and waiting to do it right doesn't warrant the assumption that I'm not willing to put in copious amounts of effort as soon, and as instantaneously, as the circumstances may dictate. In the meanwhile, sit still and be quiet.

In the beach community where we've chosen to live, there seems to be a niche for any of life's wanderers who want to settle and add to the community. Even for one such as myself who seems to lack a glaring attribute other than "he surfs real pretty," the community seems satisfied that the attribute that you do possess may well be laudable but a bit more subtle than the casual observer may be willing to recognize. Sitting and waiting with a good attitude for long periods of time in complete silence is an attribute and very often the surest path to success while in the role of a predator. And, no, you cannot pay someone to do the sitting and waiting for you if you expect to be in on the success when it finally occurs.

So I sit and watch and pay attention and try to figure out when and where to place myself so that I end up in the path of those singular moments of blinding success! For me, those singular moments are worth sitting and waiting for a seeming eternity to allow that moment to unfold. So I sit for hours…and hours… And, sure as you please, I've managed to market my limited skill set and find an occupation/lifestyle that has supported us for three and a half decades. Ironically, most of my success is due entirely to my ability to do absolutely nothing but just sit and look around for, quite literally, years' worth of days, maybe even decades' worth. Go figure! I was born to be a guide, I reckon.

Of course, please also remember that the blind you just had the hunt of a lifetime in didn't build itself on that location, nor did the dozen other blinds the guide opted not to hunt that day, and the brush that so effectively concealed your presence in all twelve blinds had to be cut, transported, and effectively affixed to the blinds. Then there's the matter that somebody had to somehow pay for and maintain the outboard motors, the boats, decoys, decoy lines and their lead weights, numerous pairs of boots, rain gear, dogs, guns, shot gun shells, thermoses, GPSs, depth finders, jack plates, boat batteries, battery cables, steering cables, trim tabs, boat registrations, boat numbers, duck blind licenses, bow lights, stern lights, Q-beams, a ten dollar guide license, your membership to Ducks Unlimited. All of these things had to be dealt with and in place for you to be in the right place at the right time with That Guy who had the blind, the equipment, and the knowledge of what to do with it all.

Also, and this isn't a minor consideration, if That Guy had to be doing something else to make a living, he wouldn't be free to have taken you on that day of days. For you to have the chance to be gunning his spot on the day of the year with the guy, either he or his outfitter would have had to have answered and returned hundreds of phone calls over the past several months. Mailings had to be written, laid out, printed, addressed, stamped, and posted. Advertising has been planned out and paid for. Return clientele doesn't just happen, so the guide/outfitter has catered to the disgruntled, the disappointed, the just generally cranky, and occasionally the truly psychotic over the last umpteen years. He's had to comp hunts to outdoor writers and make hotel and dinner reservations; he's made countless car arrangements and has provided rides for clients who expect to hunt, but, for whatever reason, don't have a vehicle at their disposal and they don't want to rent one. He's had to buy dinner for whole groups of guys for myriads of reasons over the years. For example, one of our groups of six guys got busted and had all of their brand new Christmas present shotguns confiscated for legally hunting in a float blind off of a senator's house (who shall go nameless) whose wife didn't like the noise of the guns, I suppose. She liked to feed wild ducks and couldn't be bothered with the fact that particular activity is against the law. She called up the chain of command among game wardens until the fact that she was a senator's wife had the desired effect and that officer went out and arrested the guys, took their guns, and made them all return from their homes in South Carolina to go to court a month later...all so the judge could throw the case out of court.

I guess what I'm trying to say is that there's a bit more to doing nothing than most are aware of.

KISSED A UNICORN AND WASN'T AWARE

11/21/1962: The Navy had recently transferred Vern to the Charleston, South Carolina, area, and in his explorations he had wittingly taken a short detour to water fowling's dark side. He'd succumbed to what I'd have to refer to as a little bit of poaching fever. The situation just kind of evolved, and even from a perspective of fifty years into the future, one can't really blame him.

It was opening weekend of the 1962/63 gunning season. He had hunted the evening of the twentieth on Lake Moultrie along the edge of a refuge. It had drizzled rain all afternoon, and he and his buddy Steve had only marginal success. The best chance they had involved a flock of teal that pitched perfectly to their decoys. They knew the teal pitched perfectly because they had ample opportunity to watch the flight into and out of range because their guns lay out of reach, ten feet away. They ended up the evening with a couple mergansers and a coot.

The following morning Vern brought another friend, Paul, back to the same spot. The day dawned to a heavy overcast, and then it seemed that the clouds simply lowered until they found themselves gunning in a dense fog till they quit at noon. They managed to rag out a single high-flying pintail, which sailed off after being hit and couldn't be found. They also shot a grebe to give Vern's little Springer Spaniel, Vip, some work.

Being that the gunning was slow, they decided to do a little exploring and soon found themselves a spot on the Cooper River looking across a small dike into a privately owned and protected open rice field — an open rice field fairly crawling with fat, feeding widgeon! "Well, well, what have we here?"

Vern hadn't seen or even heard another shot booming in the distance in the two days he'd been hunting, and he knew that even if somebody did venture out, nobody could see or hear much in the thickness of the fog. The day had gotten warmer, hinting that the weather was about to clear and any birds that might've flown probably wouldn't once it did. As such, there really wasn't much reason for anybody else to venture out onto the river this late on a Sunday afternoon. Did I mention that the rice field on the other side of the little dike was alive with peeping widgeon and that more were falling into the field all the while? Hmm....

In their guilty haste they missed the wind in relation to the point they had decided to hunt and pretty well bungled their decoy placement. They committed the fatal error of making the decoying fowl have to fly across the land in order to get into their decoys. In Vern's own words written in his "Remarks" column for that day and represented in the map he drew showing how the decoys were placed, he realized the error: "...hundreds of birds using the field! Mostly baldpates...threw decoys out in a hurry and birds would land every place but in the spread!"

For the evening, Vern managed to harvest four coot and — wait for it now — two European Widgeon! He noted the harvesting of four coot and two European Widgeon and didn't even realize the rarity of his accomplishment. In the rest of his life, Vern never had another shot at a widgeon of the European variety.

In the fifty years that I've been water fowling, I've only had one whack at a European widgeon that I was aware of, which I whiffed! I could easily see his rust-colored head and the extra white in the bird's scapulars shining in the afternoon sun. I whiffed on the first shot and then my gun's barrel got snarled up in some brush nailed to my duck blind. I just had to stand there and watch my one and only half-century's worth of gunning opportunity at a Euro wing away.

And he writes in the "Birds" column for that date: four coot and two European widgeon...no exclamation points... no capitalization or underlining! Ho, hum. Maybe tomorrow I'll shoot three grebes and a couple spectacled eiders, or maybe a ruddy and a black-bellied whistling duck, or how about a couple hen mergansers and a pair of drake harlequin ducks. Sheez!

DUCK RUMAKI

Since 2013 will be my fiftieth year harvesting wild duck, one could properly assume that I've eaten a pile of fowl. Of all the recipes for cooking wild duck that I've been privileged to have sampled, one recipe stands apart from all the rest in terms of reliably excellent taste, ease in all stages of preparation and near total lack of effort involved in post-meal clean up.

Photo courtesy Troy Cranford.

The recipe is called Duck Rumaki, although it's also perfect with dove breasts. Try it once, and from that day onward, you'll eat roughly ninety-eight percent of all your wild water fowl this way. Usually, at this point in a conversation about cooking, I'd have Ellen take over, but Duck Rumaki is so simple even a simple guy can do it, and I may be as simple as any guy alive.

Remember, everything about this recipe is easy, so to begin with, do not pluck your duck. Instead, feel the belly of the duck and find the bottom of the rib bones at the top of the bird's belly. Right where the two meet, pinch the bird's skin and feathers and use a sharp knife to make a slit big enough to get a couple of finger tips in. Once you get a finger from each hand in the slit, peel the skin (and, subsequently, the feathers) to either side and up into the neck, exposing all the breast meat.

The breast is made up of two halves separated by a bone that resembles a boat's keel when all the meat is removed. The keel runs from under the bird's chin to the base of the ribs. Just slice down, along either side of the keel until you hit bone and have to stop. Now grab either side of the breast meat and pull it away toward the wing while filleting the meat away from the bone. Repeat on the other side.

Congratulations! You have now filleted the breast meat off of a duck. Rinse the meat really well while being extra careful to clean out any coagulated blood and to poke a finger into any pellet holes to make sure the pellet is not there, nor that any feathers got pulled into the wound with the pellet.

Now you'll want to cut each breast half into bite-sized pieces. Soak these pieces for a couple of hours in a marinade of teriyaki sauce mixed with a bit of freshly grated ginger.

Take a one-pound package of bacon and cut it in half so that all the bacon pieces are about five inches long. Lay each piece of bacon on a cutting board, and lay one chunk of duck and a slice of water chestnut on each bacon slice. Roll each bacon/duck/chestnut slice up and run each roll-up onto a skewer. Each roll-up is a Duck Rumaki. You should be able to get about six or seven rumakis onto each skewer. Don't forget to soak your skewers so they don't burn up while cooking.

Finally, throw all of your rumaki-laden skewers onto an outdoor grill and cook until the bacon is done. And that's it! Your entrée is finished.

We usually serve our rumakis with two sides. One is Ellen's pasta, vegetable and mayonnaise salad, and the other is some sliced tomatoes mixed with balsamic vinaigrette and a bit of fresh basil.

Bon apetit!

Pasta Salad,
ELLEN STYLE

Now that Vic's given you the recipe for rumakis, here's my pasta salad recipe.

INGREDIENTS:
1 box of penne or shell pasta
1-1/2 to 2 cups mayonaise
1 red onion, diced
1 green pepper, seeded and diced
1 red pepper, seeded and diced
1 tomato diced, or a bunch of cherry tomatoes halved
1 cucumber, peeled and chopped into bite sized pieces
3 stalks celery, chopped
1 tablespoon each, basil
Salt and pepper to taste
1 teaspoon thyme leaves

Cook pasta and drain. Add remaining ingredients. Voila!

Photo courtesy Vic Berg.

I MEAN IT...
THAT'S IT!

I just counted all the fowl shot by clients of Outer Banks Waterfowl from our foundation in 1977 until the end of the 2011/12 season. My total will be off by several hundred, as I didn't get a full accounting of all fowl harvested during the three years when I had tried to shift ownership to another outfitter back in the early 1990s. That didn't work out so well, so I regained ownership and have run the service to the present day.

Photo courtesy Joe Law.

Since OBW's inception in 1977 till the end of the 2012 season, the guide service has taken 19,945 fowl. Our average take is up over a thousand fowl per year. Fifteen to twenty percent of those are drake pintail, even though we harvest around twenty-five different species per season. You just never know what you're going to see next, but there's a good chance that they're going to be pintail.

Every season, Ellen and I swear to each other that this is it. We are not going to hire any additional guides or grow any bigger! But, of course, just then we run across another guy with great equipment, awesome blind locations and years of professional guide experience. Last year we added two more excellent guides, and we're now up to thirteen. But, I mean it, that's it!

"Ah, the Quirks of the Guides"

Number one, and above any other consideration, an outfitter is nothing without his guides. While totally cognizant of this fact, a good outfitter very often has to sell quirks as attributes if he is to have a chance at staying in the business.

In the counties where we live and hunt, the duck blind laws favor blind locations over a willing guide's aptitude and hunting skills because all of the duck blind locations are grandfather-claused to their present owner and his/her heirs. If you get a blind in your name, it stays yours forever as long as you build, brush and hunt the location even only once in any duck season.

If you give this matter any thought, it's not long before you realize that the skills of the guide are secondary to his ability to own good duck blind locations. As such, there is a temptation to hire less than adequate guides who control better than average blind locations. Thankfully, over the decades we've ended up representing the good guides with the good locations. This wasn't always the case.

Being a preacher's kid, I spent a few weeks of every summer in what was known as Vacation Bible School. Of course, it wasn't a vacation to us kids, but neither was it an elective. I'm pretty sure the vacation was for the Moms. As I remember it, most of what one did in a Presbyterian's vacation Bible school was listen to and talk about Bible stories.

Maybe it was that the teachers were volunteer Moms and Dads and not properly trained in advanced, religiously founded mind control, or maybe it was that lots of religion is faith based, and faith, as a noun, is really tricky to illustrate and pin down; it's especially difficult to try to teach to quizzical and inquisitive six-year-olds.

Interestingly, our Presbyterian elders felt that the best way to teach advanced philosophical truths to its infant members was through stories that had key bits of information mysteriously withheld. We, as kids, were supposed to take these incomplete sets of information and, after much discussion, were supposed to deduce the very tenets that our religion was founded on. These stories were called parables.

Unfortunate for parables is that the foundation for the tenet that we were supposed to deduce was based on a principle of faith. Once again, unfortunately, a principle of faith is, by definition, based on an assumption. Assumption, of course, is another word for best guess. And once you arrive at best guess, you eventually are left to ponder who the best guess would best serve. I believe the best guesser has the most invested in the conversation.

One of the more inexplicable Bible stories centered on Moses, his starving people and manna from heaven. The biggest problem I had with the story was that nobody could or would tell me what manna was. All we do know is that it comes from heaven. Hmm.

Oh, come on now. Somebody knows more than that! Was manna a paste or meat on a bone, bugs and grubs eaten in desperation or something else entirely? I'm just saying that if historians knew as much as they do about the story of manna from heaven that some mention of its consistency would be found somewhere. I don't know what conspiracy would have to be at play for it to be important enough to leave this bit of information from the human record, but the fact that it was gives me foundation enough to doubt the information organized religion does decide to share. The best I could ever get to an answer was another question.

"Well, what do you think manna was?"

"What? How should I know?" I was only a six year old kid. If pressed I'd probably express a leaning toward an alien staple…or energy bars from an advanced Us. It could have been insects, locusts maybe. People can eat insects. Bugs have lots of protein.

Fifty years into the future, and thinking referenced to a lifetime as an outdoor guide, I think I may have figured out what manna is.

Buffleheads! Go figure, but who knows? What I do know is that for three months out of every year, the lowly, low-flying buffleheads provide a good portion of many family's monetary and dietary needs.

On slow weather days, what duck guide hasn't counted on the dippers, as the locals refer to them, to bail out a decent shoot. Throw a few dozen, fat, freshly harvested oysters into a game bag already stuffed full of limits of drake buffleheads and I'll show you a feast on the hoof.

Having said all of this, however, please be warned that a blessing is often easily morphed into a curse. The problem with buffleheads is that they're too easy. At times, it's way too easy. What happens when a guide realizes that even with bad/average shots in the blind, he can be limited out most mornings by seven-thirty… and you really don't even need to set out but eight to ten decoys…at the most…and he gets paid the same as the guide who put out 120 decoys and hunted till dark for a shot at some "good" ducks. Whoa.

I call it "going to the dark side" when a guide quits giving a rat's behind about hunting puddle ducks and begins gauging his success by how early he could get his guys limited out and back to the docks. About the time I hear that the guide isn't even carrying his gun with him anymore — because he doesn't want his party to have any reason to think that they can shoot his limit too — is when I know that the guide's ambition and pride are done. As soon as I can cover his parties, he is too.

Of course, I had to learn how to be a hard ass about it, but in my defense, I've been buffle-lowed before. If these guys weren't done and packing up by sunrise, they were getting bitchy quick.

Now don't get me wrong, there are days when the big ducks just are not going to fly and the gun club across from me has rigged out four dipper blinds. All four club blinds are hammering away at the buffs, so you may as well tie out your own buffle palace location and join in the massacre as the somewhat dim-witted fowl bounce from decoy spread to decoy spread like pin-balls with a death wish. The more confusion and chaos present within sight and earshot, the better for shooting dippers.

On days that you are on the downwind end of the shooting flats, all the percussion from all the shots makes it nearly impossible to land decoying puddlers without them being flared by somebody shooting upwind. At this point you may as well join in the chaos as grumble about it. On days when you're the farthest upwind, however, you're in a virtual sound vacuum because all the noise is being blown away from you. When this is the case, decoying puddlers aren't getting spooked by the sound of gunfire from other gunners. On these days, you should be concentrating on big ducks. I don't care who they are, most paying hunters would rather shoot pintail and widgeon over buffleheads and mergansers.

To gun dippers on days that big ducks are available, just so you can go home and go back to bed, is just wrong. Wrong and lazy! Once again, if dippers are all you got, then get after 'em. But, you'd best be looking for access to big duck blinds if you want to get consistent bookings. And, even if you know that all you're going to shoot on a given day is dippers, at least put out a spread of decoys…and bring your gun…and some duck calls…and your enthusiasm.

All my guides are enthusiastic gunners on their own. Most are truly professional outdoorsmen who love to hunt. I encourage these traits. I truly cannot fathom a service where the guides are treated more shabbily than kennel dogs. There's a service up the road from me that, when they construct their duck blinds — and they have more than fifty — they build a walled box to sit in but extend the seat out into space beyond the box. That's where the guide is expected to sit. In blinds that don't have the bench extended into space, the guide is expected to spend the day sitting in the boat that is stashed in a covered boat hide. Yeah, right. I guess, from a guide's point of view, if a guy is willing to treat you like this in the first place, it's probably for the best that you're relieved of the necessity to make small talk all day.

I have guys that won't quite go so far as to call me "boy," but it's a conscious decision not to. We don't usually get along.

Ruddy Pot Pie

Ruddy pot pie is a traditional recipe that was created out of necessity back at the turn of the century. In the old days, ruddy ducks were second only to canvasbacks when cost per pair was considered and were known as "dollar ducks," as they sold for a dollar a pair. Twenty-pound swans brought about thirty cents a pair. The smaller ruddy was considered a delicacy whose texture, tenderness and taste made it perfectly suited for inclusion in a pot pie, as you could stretch a small amount of the duck with veggies from the garden and pie crust and feed a family generously. This is my adaptation of the recipe.

INGREDIENTS:

1 box Pillsbury® Pie crusts
   (usually next to biscuits in refrigerated section of grocers)
2-3 duck breasts cut into bite sized pieces
1 cup flour
Salt and pepper
3 cloves garlic, minced
1/2 cup corn, frozen or fresh
1/2 cup peas, frozen or fresh
1/2 cup carrots, diced
1/2 cup chopped onion
1 sweet pepper, seeded and diced
1 beef bouillon cube
1 chicken bouillon
1-1/2 cup water
1/2 teaspoon thyme
1/2 teaspoon rosemary
1/2 teaspoon tarragon
1 teaspoon basil leaves
1/2 teaspoon coarse ground pepper
Salt to taste

Photo courtesy
Troy Cranford.

Prepare pie crust as directed for 2-crust pie. Dredge duck pieces in flour. Melt butter in large skillet, brown duck pieces. Add onions, carrots and sweet pepper and sauté. Add remaining ingredients and simmer till thickened. You may need to add a mixture of one tablespoon flour with 1/2-tablespoon butter to aid in thickening. Pour mixture into pie crust. Top with crust, seal edges with fork or fingers and poke top with fork. Bake at 375 degrees for 1 hour. Let rest for 5-10 minutes before cutting.

THE BASIC-EST OF THE BASICS

At the very heart of the hunting experience lies the unmistakable fact that this activity focuses unyielding attention on life's most basic instincts. Your intent is to kill and eat so that you can continue to live.

Bam! It doesn't get any simpler; we're animals, get used to it. Better yet, get better at it.

The more you hunt, the more you realize that getting complicated usually goes counter to your best interests. Simpler is better. I defy anybody to show me a more consistent way to catch fish than by floating live bait under a bobber — no nets, please, as that's a different matter entirely. So is dynamite….To catch a fish, just feed it what it already wants to eat precisely when it wants to eat it; just add a hook and a line. Hunting is that simple as well. You just have to already be where your prey wants to go at any moment in time.

I think the most consistent flaw that keeps an outdoorsman from success afield is over-thinking situations. With that being said, I think the second-most consistent flaw leading to non-success afield is in not understanding and respecting the basics associated with the "animal-ness" of the endeavor you are involved in. The critters you are after don't want to get killed and eaten. You disagree and put all your efforts into imposing your will…only to find out that imposing your will doesn't usually work out the way you thought it might, and you actually harvest less game.

As compensation, most individuals become more studious and diligent — and they invest vaster increments of time and finances into capturing their quarry. This, oddly enough, still seems to have the opposite effect than they'd hoped, and they capture even less game on average than before. Usually, at this point many would-be outdoorsmen get discouraged, quit hunting, and take up texting or trying to understand women or some other contrivance to kill time. What the would-be outdoorsmen never contemplated was the basic-est of the basics whose main tenet could be summed up simply: Keep it simple!

In all situations, the simpler answer is the correct one as long as both options are effective. You don't need a $35,000-dollar bass boat with twin 200s mounted on jack plates with power trim if a fourteen-foot aluminum skiff with a twenty horse-power outboard gets you the same number of ducks in as safe a manner.

As long as you are safe, the simpler is better. Keep making decisions in this manner, and soon you'll be lean and mean. Besides, if you save enough on one boat, you may be able to afford another and two boats are always better than one.

Let me illustrate the level of simple or basic that we're shooting for. The question that I'd like answered is: What is the most important thing you need to have in order to experience an epic duck hunt?

Real quick, list the top five to ten things you most need to have to consistently shoot more ducks, with the emphasis on consistently. I'll wait. Don't read ahead. Go ahead and make a list.

Yes, it's obvious that you need a good shotgun because, without it, you can't even shoot at a duck, and you also need good, maintained decoys to even get the birds into range, and without a good boat and reliable motor you couldn't even get to the blind. And then there's the blind and blind location; take, for example, Pintail Point. On most days it'll outshoot most any (unbaited) blind locations.

None of these are the right answers, though, because if the birds don't fly on any given day, none of these things will make a whit of difference. What is most important is a reason for birds to fly and move around in the first place. So, weather is the answer?

No. Weather is an incomplete answer as is the wind, the tide, cold, or ice (although a developing ice-up would be a good second place answer). No, the one thing that most assuredly gets birds moving is falling barometric pressure.

Birds are acutely aware of what a barometer illustrates and are affected by its swings in seeming species-wide mood shifts. The barometric pressure goes up and the weather will clear. As a result, birds get lazy, find a comfortable spot out of the wind, and they go to sleep. They don't even seem to need to eat. If a persistent high pressure system settles in, fowl can literally sleep for days.

On the other hand, if the barometric pressure falls, birds wake up, and they get skittish. It's as if energy is being created. Wherever they are just doesn't seem right to them, and they start moving around, looking for food. I think they move around and eat so much because they can tell by the pressure that the weather is going to deteriorate and the winds will increase, but they can't tell in advance how bad it's going to get. It may get so extreme that it may be hard to find food at all, so they stock up.

The most glaring example of this phenomenon that I've witnessed occurred during the approach of one of the hurricanes that I've been overridden by over the years. Maybe it was Felix or Isabelle or Gustav. I don't remember which; there have been so many.

The hurricane was approaching, landfall was imminent. Ellen and I had decided to leave the bird feeders hanging as long as we possibly could because our deck birds seemed starved.

It's not an accident that Ellen and I have one of the most secure hurricane houses on the beach, even though our doorstep is less than a mile from the ocean. We live on a ridge that runs through an ancient maritime forest. We're totally tucked under a dense canopy of strong hardwood trees and behind a high dune ridge that runs between us and the ocean.

While we are tucked under and behind a formidable natural protector, our house is also perched atop a secondary, lower ridge line that also puts us above any potential flooding. Our house is the house that thirty- and forty-year residents of the beach come to when we need to ride out the scariest storms. We never evacuate!

As the hurricane neared landfall, virtually at our doorstep, the hysteria from every television station had become such a homogenous spate of doom-saying blather that we had finally muted Jim "We're All Gonna Die!" Cantore in mid-harangue and cranked up the music, figuring we might as well enjoy some tunes up till when the power went out. We actually run cash pools paid out to whoever most closely predicts the exact time that the power and/or cable goes out.

Oddly enough with this hurricane, neither the power nor the cable went out at all, and I was able to closely observe the barometer on the weather channel as Jim "We're All Gonna Die!" pantomimed fear and horror, silently, in time with Maria Muldaur, who at the time was crooning on our sound system, "Time is something that money can't repay."

It was then that I noticed the birds on our deck; there were more and they were hungry. For the next few hours, I watched the birds feeding in relation to the tumble the barometer was recording.

Just a quick aside for anyone who doesn't live in hurricane territory: A hurricane isn't imminent the same way that a tornado is imminent. Hurricanes don't do anything quickly. You've been hearing about the big, destructive, lumbering oaf since it formed up off of the western tip of Africa a week and a half ago, and with the same trepidation one awaits the arrival of the in-laws for a summer vacation at your house, you sit and wait for the hurricane to finally arrive and proceed with the requisite ass-whooping.

A normal barometer reading would be around thirty point zero. Thirty point anything is tending to run high, and the skies clear and the world is pretty. Twenty-nine point anything is a low reading, and the skies are going to cloud, and the lower it gets, the more unsettled the weather is going to get. If a barometer reads in the twenty-eight point range, you are probably in a hurricane and are presently receiving your ass-whooping. At this point the world is very much not pretty.

The barometer on the weather channel read twenty-eight point seven three. A big tree limb cracked, broke, and nearly took out the bird feeders. That, I expected.

What I didn't expect was that the birds were not only not going away and seeking shelter, but they were amassing in greater numbers and eating more and more. Essentially, in the three hours that the barometer was in the twenty-eight point range, the birds ate in three hours what they usually ate in three days!

Whenever anybody asks about when the best time to hunt is, the most accurate answer would be that the best time to hunt is during a falling barometer.

The second best mover of ducks is ice — which can get real extreme — and your third best friend is wind, usually from the north. Of course, there is one element that can, and very often does, trump all other physical phenomena, and that is just plain old, simple-ass luck. Some got it and some just don't seem to. The only reason that I may win out in most any situation is perseverance and guile. I can be sneaky. It also doesn't hurt to hang out with somebody who is lucky...Just so you can see what it looks like.

WILLIAM'S TRANSCENDENTAL DUCK HUNT

"What do you mean, you don't want to hunt with Marvin?" I was talking to William, a good friend who started gunning with us during the second year of OBW's existence.

Photo courtesy Chris Price.

"I'd just rather not," William replied. I knew something was going on when William was terse. As of the instant when I write this sentence, William has hunted with our guides several times a season, every season, for better than three decades. I believe in my heart that William has used every guide who ever worked for OBW. He brought corporate groups of eight to ten clients per trip for a couple decades straight, so I was interested in what he had to say. It also didn't hurt that William is wickedly perceptive. If he had a problem with one of my guides, I wanted to hear about it from him. I knew for a fact that I could count on William to be painstakingly honest in his assessments because he is incapable of lying or exaggerating. Well, not so much incapable as just not interested in lying or exaggerating. When you're as quickly astute as William is, it's just so much more refreshing and, well, just so much more interesting when you always deal from a position of point-blank honesty.

"All right, what's Marvin done that's stuck in your craw?" I ask. "Spill it."

William looked me square in the eye, "Have you ever hunted with him?" still with the eye contact.

I squirmed a bit, "No," I had to answer truthfully. Marvin had been working for us for a couple of years. He'd come to us, recommended by somebody, but I couldn't remember who exactly, and this was back in the hooligan days. We've had some guides who were real characters. Marvin was real good about being on time in the wee hours every morning, and his clients shot good numbers of fowl most days, so I hadn't been aware to keep an eye on him. I had noticed that his clients seemed to be limiting out on bufflehead seemingly earlier and earlier every day, and I kind of had been wondering why he didn't seem to be shooting big ducks like he'd used to.

"Are you aware of his boat?"

"What? Oh, you mean the red sparkly bass boat with the big honkin' motor? Yeah, he told me about that. He said his boat broke — those were his words exactly, although I never knew what he meant by his boat breaking — and he had to borrow the bass boat. Marvin said it wasn't an issue, though, because his boat hide is so thickly brushed. Why? Is his boat flaring ducks?" I asked helpfully.

"I think Marvin wants it to flare ducks," was William's incongruous reply.

"What?" I asked, truly not understanding. "Why would he want to flare ducks?" That didn't make any sense.

"Probably to strike horror in the hearts of all the buffleheads," was William's snappish reply. "It really doesn't matter how well a boat hide is brushed up if the boat's never in it," he continued, his arms crossed. William's eyes held their grip on my own eyes. He had stopped talking. I knew he was waiting for me now. Waiting for me to say something naïve so he'd have a reason to enlighten me. I couldn't help but oblige.

With slow understanding, I ask the question, "So, he's running the boat to stir up the ducks?"

"Bingo, but not ducks so much as buffleheads," was the quick retort. Again, William waited, arms crossed, the solid stare.

"And...Marvin really seems to like driving the sparkly red bass boat with the big honkin' motor?" I surmise.

"Again, bingo! But he only drives it wide-screaming open."

"And Marvin is really pushing you to limit on the buffs so he can get his ass back home and back into bed," I concluded in a rush of understanding.

"Victor, I must say that you are on a roll. Bingo again."

I know William real well, and I also know how he likes to hunt. He is an all-day hunter and, as such, he's willing to wait for shots at big ducks. Unless the day is going to be blue-birdy and slow, he'll usually pass on the buffleheads altogether. On the other hand, William is usually so easy to get along with that I had already organized the entire other fourteen two-man groups who were to hunt the following day. The dread that realizing how screwed I really was began to sink in.

"Is there anything else?" I had been afraid to ask the question, but I figured I may as well get all of the bad news out of the way.

"Have you been in his blind?" William asked quietly.

"No. Why?" I had a feeling I knew the answer. Our hotel had a deal with the hunters who stayed there, and they provided each hunter with a box lunch for their day afield. Box lunch was not a euphemism. Each man who hunted got a heavy, wax coated, orange checkered paper lunch box that contained the following food items: two pieces of fried chicken, two sandwiches (I use the term sandwich in its most liberal definition, as one of the sandwiches was two slices of bread swiped at with a mayonnaise-slathered knife, topped with one slice of American cheese food product, and the other sandwich was two slices of bread flanking a perfunctory swath of pimento cheese spread), a slice of dill pickle, two hard-boiled eggs and a package of three or four Oreo cookies.

Each of these food items was individually wrapped in wax paper, so all of these wrappings when undone and added to the orange and white checker colored wax box, which by now had unfolded itself , along with the chicken bones, the egg shells and very often the pimento cheese sandwiches combined to make a sizeable pile of trash. Now times that pile of trash by two men and multiply that pile of garbage by a couple weeks' worth of clients, and blinds have been known to get out of control trashy.

"Has Marvin let his blind get trashed up with the box lunches? I try and tell all the guides to keep trash bags in their boats. I'll give him some myself," I offered preemptively.

"Yeah, his blind is a mess," William shot back, "the last time I was in it, I brought my own trash bags, but that only made things worse."

"Why? Was the blind full of cormorant shit under all the garbage or something?"

"No, that would be easy to fix. You can kick bird poop out of a blind with your rubber boots. I've done that before. I'll ask you again, have you been in his blind?"

"No," I mumbled.

"Then I guess you don't know about the channel markers."

"The what? What can channel markers have to do with a duck blind?" I asked. "Did one of them wash ashore near the blind? Are the reflective red or green numbers shining and flaring the ducks? Couldn't somebody just flip the sign over so that it doesn't shine?"

"The answers to your questions are, the channel markers, they are the blind; I don't know where he got them; yes they are flaring the ducks; and you'd have to flip the whole blind over."

William's answers made no sense. "William, what are you talking about?" I had to ask.

"They are the floor," was the answer. "The knucklehead used the channel markers to make the floor of his blind — one red one and one green. You should see the glow when the sun gets up a bit. It's so bright in the blind from the day-glow numbers and background coloring that they make the signs out of that when the sun hits them, I swear there's an aurora around the blind." William is finally laughing at the absurdity. I'm flummoxed.

"Why did he put 'em face up?" I asked.

"Who knows what Marvin is thinking? I did ask him though. He said the glow shouldn't matter, because we should be gone by the time the sun comes up. Right about then a hen bufflehead flew by. When we didn't reach for our guns quickly enough, he grabbed his, killed the buff, told us that duck was on our limits, and he roared across the sound in his sparkly red bass boat with its big honkin' motor. It is effective," William continued without missing a beat. "That boat with that motor scares all hell out of the buffs. To change the subject," William continued, warming to his topic, "I'm guessing that if you've never gunned with Marvin, then you probably haven't seen his dog work?"

"No," I answered.

"You're not missing anything," William went on, "he sucks as a retriever. The dog's a pretty lab, but he's real timid. I don't think the dog much cares for jumping into cold water."

"He doesn't abuse the dog, does he?" I was concerned because I know William will not abide anybody mishandling their retriever.

"No, not technically," William answered cryptically. "You know that I'm usually on the dog's side, but in this case, the dog pretty much deserved it, and he never got hurt."

"What?"

"You know how big Marvin is," William continued. "What is he? Six-three, six-four, and with that big belly, he's got to weigh at least 320 or better. Well, the last time I hunted with him, there finally came a point where he had that fat, hundred-pound house pet held at full stretch over his head...."

"Holy! He what?"

William had me in his gaze again. "Let me tell you about my last hunt with Marvin. Gee, I don't even know where to start..." he paused a second, gazing at an empty space a foot and a half over and to the left of the top of my head as he collected his recollections. Suddenly, his eyes lowered and I was locked in his stare again.

"I guess the place to start would be at the dock at Pirate's Cove where we met him in the morning. Marvin was good. Punctual. Good attitude. You'd almost have to say, professional."

"Phew," I let it slip.

"Yeah, that's where that ended," William snapped in response. "Then he led us to the sparkly red bass boat with the big honkin' motor." William had added it as an aside, almost a bit in awe because, if nothing else, William is a big fan of verve.

"You should see that boat shine in the glare of a million candle-power spotlight," he aped squinting and shielding his eyes. "Really, Vic, it was so bright it almost made Dave's and my eyes bleed!"

William continued, "I looked at Dave, and Dave looked at me. We'd been hunting together down here for about fifteen years at that point, so we figured, how bad could it be? We've decided to not make decisions based on that criterion any more. Marvin mumbled something about his boat being broke and how he was able to borrow this beauty. He said it like it was a good thing, so we believed him. Better a sparkly red bass boat with a big honkin' motor that works than a so-called broken boat, so Dave and I went about getting our stuff out of the truck. All of a sudden Marvin came running up, "Hold it right there! What's with all the camping gear boys? We're not going camping today. You guys are going to limit and be back here at the dock before you could even use half that stuff."

William knew where this story was going, so he let slip a little chuckle. "What ensued at that point," William continued, "was the first time we exchanged words that day. The end point of that discussion was that nobody knows what's going to happen, so we took all of our stuff. Marvin wasn't happy, and he's not shy about showing it."

William began to warm to his story. We're talking at the bar of the Sea Ranch hotel where nearly all of my hunting clients stay. I had thought I was about done for the night, being that my last client was William, but I could see this story wasn't near over and I was going to have to undo and redo some of the organizing that had almost been completed. Oh, well. I ordered another drink when the bartender walked by.

"So the next thing," William went on, "Dave and I are in the boat. Bradda, bradda..." William bellowed, imitating the sound of Marvin's big honkin' motor. "As we're pulling away from the dock, Marvin's spotlight quit working. He whacked the light against the steering console a couple of times in an attempt to bully the light into working then gave up and threw the light over the side of the boat. 'Screw it,' Marvin says over the bradda bradda bradda thrum of the motor. 'I can see in the dark better without the light anyway. Let's run the ditch.'

"About this time," William intoned, "was when Dave and I figured we were done for. When Marvin threw down on the throttle, that red sparkly bass boat nearly leapt out of the water! Bwaaaaa!" William very nearly screamed. His animation in telling the story was beginning to attract the attention of the other hunters still in the bar, and a crowd was gathering. William didn't seem to notice as he continued, shouting over the imagined scream of the big honkin' motor.

"When Marvin pegged the throttle on that big honkin' motor, we went from zero to nearly seventy in an instant. All of a sudden, Dave and I finally got what 'tears in your ears' meant." William swung around and looked into my eyes from mere inches away. "Did you know that is a literal phenomenon?" William nearly whispered. "At a certain

141

speed — I believe just prior to breaking the sound barrier — your eyes tear up and the wind in your face drives them right into your ears." He was playing to the crowd now and they were eating it up.

"Bwaaaah!!" William screamed again, imitating the big honkin' motor. He pretended almost falling backward off of his bar stool as he clung to the bar with his fingertips. "This would have been more than enough," William screamed over the imaginary rush of the wind in his face as he aped wiping away the imaginary pool of tears collecting in his ears, "if Marvin had stayed in the channel around to the mouth of Broad Creek where his blind is. But, noooo! No sooner were we up to speed than Marvin snatched the steering wheel to the right and we headed for the mouth of John's Ditch."

"Aaaaaagh!" William made the scream echo the sound of a horrified little girl. "There's a reason that little snaky, switch-back riddled little creek is called a ditch," William nearly cried, trying to both cover his eyes and peak through his fingers. "The sedge grass that lines the ditch is twice taller than a man, and the creek itself isn't more than ten, fifteen feet wide for nearly a mile," William explained to the crowd as he pitched and yawed around on his bar stool as he clung desperately to the bar top. "Aaaaaagh!" he screamed again, sounding like the terrified little girl. "Suddenly, we're skidding to a stop in front of our blind. It seemed that we covered the two miles to the blind in roughly fourteen seconds…I'm not sure we didn't access a worm-hole," William concluded, again cracking up the crowd that was now hanging on to his every word.

"Once I caught my breath, I asked Marvin why he wasn't afraid of running into somebody coming the other way. His answer — that nobody should be driving the creek in that direction at that time of the morning — seemed to me to be the incorrect response. His next comment — that anybody driving the creek in that direction at that time in the morning should know enough not to because he (Marvin) might be coming the other way — was hardly reassuring. When I asked what about if the other guy's light broke, the same way Marvin's had, only elicited a blank stare, like I was talking Japanese or something. This, by the way, led to our second serious exchange of words," William informed me. "We decided that the next time, we'd

drive past John's ditch and continue along the main boat channel until we could turn into the 300-yard-wide mouth of Broad Creek where his blind is," William finished. He stood, looking at me with a "Well?" look in his eyes.

Inexorably, I rise to the bait, "Well, that had to be a scary ride, in the dark and all," I offered sympathetically.

"No, Victor, scary is meeting a very large man in your doctor's waiting room dressed as Cher, for Halloween, and finding out that he'll be the physician performing your proctologic exam," William interjected to the delight of the gathering crowd. He continued, "Did I mention that I was sitting in the fishing chair that's mounted way forward on the bow for the whole ride?" William asked pointedly.

I revised my interpretation of what that horrific ride must have been like, running the narrow, serpentine ditch, mounted on a seat that was bolted onto the forward deck a mere three feet from the pointy tip of the boat's bow. "Oh," was all that my mouth could offer.

"Yeah! Oh!" William muttered, changing the subject "Marvin's decoy rig, how big is it?"

"I don't know," I had to admit.

"Go ahead and guess," William shot back.

I figured he was setting me up, so I guessed low. "I don't know, twenty, twenty-five decoys?" I ventured.

"Try five," he answered. "And two of those were three-quarters sunk by the time it was legal to shoot. And one of the three left didn't have any paint on it! That was the third time Marvin and I had words," William offered as an aside.

"We decided that Marvin was going to set out every decoy that was in his boat. I told him that we'd wait to start gunning until the rig was set."

"There goes limiting out by sunrise," I whistled appreciatively.

"Exactly," William averred. "If Marvin wanted to bump heads, I figured I had all day to bump heads." William chuckled a bit and then got serious again.

"Of course, his passive-aggressive response was to set the decoys by flinging them, one by one, from the shoreline."

"Oh geez," was the best I could offer. "You don't mean that he'd walk the hundred yards to the boat hide, grab an armload of decoys, walk the hundred yards back to the blind, fling those decoys into the water, then back to the boat hide…."

"Victor," William chided, "it's like you were there. It took him eight trips. I counted." William was back to enjoying the telling of his story. All the other hunters listening were transfixed. I had no idea how I was going to get anybody to hunt with Marvin now, so I did the only thing that seemed to make sense at the time…I ordered another drink.

"Do you know what made it even better?" William asked gleefully.

"I'm afraid to ask," I answered balefully.

"We were eat up with birds while Marvin was fixing the rig, and we never fired a shot," he replied while laughing.

"What?" I laughed so suddenly that I choked on the sip of whiskey I'd been nursing in my mouth. Between coughs and gasps, I managed, "You mean…Marvin had to watch… lots of shots?"

"He started it," William retorted, laughing. "You wouldn't think Marvin's face could get any redder without popping," William guffawed. "We passed on bluebills — both lesser and greater — some ring necks, some hoodies, plenty of buffs." William was whooping now. He swiped at some tears forming in the corners of his eyes.

"I thought he was going to cry when the greater blue bills coasted across the decoys a second time."

"Oh, my God! That had to have nearly killed him. What'd he say?" I asked naively.

"You wouldn't want to print it," he roared, swiping at new tears as the other hunters couldn't help but laugh along.

"Please tell me that's it," I pleaded when the bar settled down a little.

"It?" William bellowed indignantly. "We haven't talked about the dog yet. No. We're not to 'it' yet."

"Here we go…." I muttered under my breath.

William continued unabated. "Marvin finally got the rig out, such as it was, considering he'd heaved each decoy from shore."

I interrupted, "So all the decoys were too close to the blind?"

"No," William answered, "he had a way of hooking the decoy line on his finger…with his finger at the midpoint of the decoy's line halfway between the decoy and the decoy's weight…the line is hooked on his finger and the decoy and the weight are hanging together…and he just flips them. All at once! It may be because he's such a big guy or maybe because he was so mad…." William was laughing again, "You should try it out," William gasped. "You can fling 'em a mile."

"God, you're enjoying this," I offered in mock dismay.

"Just hook the line between the weight and the decoy," William intoned, ignoring me, "and flip!" His voice rose as he said it and his hands traded places in a flash. Everybody roared.

"Will it never end?" I implored to no one in particular.

"I don't know. You hired him," was the prophetic retort. Changing the subject, "So there we were. It's a good hour after shooting time. We're finally set up, guns loaded and ready to hunt…and of course the morning flight is over." William looked around the room with eyebrows raised…a "what did you expect?" expression on his face. "So it wasn't long before Marvin lost patience with waiting and nearly dove out the door. 'I'll get the birds moving,' hung in the air as Marvin made the move for his secret weapon, the sparkly red bass boat with the big honkin' motor!"

"Bradda, bradda, bradda!"

"He's started the red sparkly beast," William intoned for the audience.

"Buwaaaaah!"

"Wide open," and again the sportscaster voice "the only forward speed that Marvin knows. And there he went," William observes, right hand a salute, shielding his eyes and looking afar. "I guess the burning of petroleum calmed him because, when he finally came skidding to a halt against the shoreline forty-five minutes later, he seemed a lot more relaxed. 'So, you ready for me to pick this mess up and get us back to the dock?' were the first words out of his mouth. It took Dave and me a few seconds to adjust to the silence when he finally shut down the big honkin' motor."

"Buwaah, bradda, bradda, brup, brup, brup, brr… up…."

"We were trying (vainly) to massage our ear drums…the big honkin' motor had been wailing in the background for the entire forty-five minutes that Marvin had been gone."

"Marvin asked again if we were ready to pick our mess up. He told me that he ran up plenty of birds when he was running around," continued William. "He said that he'd seen us shoot before, and he demanded to know where our birds were. Dave and I were still rubbing our ears, trying to massage the high-pitched whine out of our heads."

"We don't have any."

At this point William started doing both sides of the conversation;

"What?" he screamed as Marvin. "What about that buff that landed in your decoys right after I left? I saw it pitch."

"Oh, yeah," William answered himself, "That one. It was a hen. We're only shooting drake buffleheads."

"What? Only drakes! Oh just shoot me in the brain!" William railed in his best Marvin voice. "Only drakes? Marvin paused a second to see if his histrionics were having any effect on me. When they didn't, he asked hopefully about the drakes he had run up. He kept insisting that he'd seen us shoot before and demanded to know where were the drakes we'd shot. I told him they floated off. I told him the last we saw, they were drifting out the mouth of the creek into the big sound."

William turned his head and answered himself in Marvin's voice, "What?"

"We knocked down four or five," William answered himself.

"What!" again as Marvin.

"Okay, maybe six."

William as Marvin: "What? Why didn't the dog get 'em? I left the dog here! Why didn't the dog get 'em?"

William: "I don't think he likes the cold water."

William as Marvin: "What?!"

William: "Or maybe the water's too choppy. Maybe the dog can't see the downed birds because the water's too choppy."

Marvin: "What?"

William: "Maybe the dog can't see, because…."

At this point William looked around the room. Assured of the entire room's rapt attention, he continued. "Right then a hen buff cut across the decoys, wings set. Marvin saw it…saw that we weren't moving for our guns…grabbed his gun…vowed that this one goes on our limit…and blasted the poor little bastard in the face at about fifteen yards. Bam! His buff hits the water, a trail of feathers forty yards beyond…then Marvin spins on the poor, unsuspecting dog… Get 'em!,' he commanded. The dog took a couple steps toward the water, stopped, looked around at us humans and wagged her tail, wondering why we were all looking at her. 'Get 'em!' again the command…the dog looked at the water and backed away from it a couple steps. 'Get 'em!' And you won't believe it. In an instant, Marvin grabbed the dog behind her head and above her tail, gave a heave and a jerk and all of a sudden has the dog under the chest and belly in both hands at full stretch over his head.

"Still can't see 'em?" William screamed in Marvin's voice. "Can you see 'em now?" He turned the dog this way and that… "How about now?" Then he heaved the poor beast into the water.

"Wow," was all I had to say.

"And, wow," William agreed. "At that point I decided that now was probably not the time to have words with Marvin for the fourth time. The dog went and got the duck, by the way, but then she went and hid it in the marsh and wouldn't show Marvin where it got hidden." With that, William totally cracked up. Everybody else in the bar paused a second, then cracked up also.

"Okay," I said after things calmed down a bit, "I can see why you don't want to …."

"I'm not done yet," William interrupted.

"Oh no," I moaned.

"Instead of having my fourth set of words with Marvin, I instead suggested that he may as well go park old Sparkly Red and join us in the blind for the rest of the morning and afternoon. He was dejected, but he finally did it," William concluded. He then caught the attention of the bartender, ordered another drink and waited for the drink to be made, all the while ignoring me and everybody else in the bar who had been hanging on his every word. Finally, I couldn't stand it anymore.

"Well?" I asked.

William looked around, seemingly surprised that I was addressing him, "Well? Well, what?"

"Well, what happened next?"

"I thought you'd never ask," he replied as he accepted his new drink from the bartender. "Not much. It was kind of sad really."

"What was sad? Did he beg to go in?"

"No, nothing that mundane. When he got back from the boat hide, he seemed like a decent, contrite human being. We chatted. We had some snacks and coffee. After about three-quarters of an hour, I looked up, and I swear, sure as I'm sitting on this bar stool, Marvin had a tear running down his big ruddy cheek. 'What's the problem?' I asked him."

"Nothing."

"No, really, what is it?"

"Well, I didn't want to be a bother, but my girlfriend's not well," Marvin explained. "She's seeing her surgeon just about right now," he continued.

William looked at me over the rim of his glass. "What were Dave and I supposed to do with that information? When we questioned Marvin a bit more, he let it slip that there was a good chance that she might not make it through the procedure."

I was surprised at this information. "That's terrible," I said, "I had no idea. What's wrong with her? I never heard about his girlfriend needing surgery." I was kind of at a loss because I truly had no idea.

"Yeah, there's a reason for that," was William's cryptic comment. Then he changed the subject. "Other than the times I've limited out, I've never voluntarily gone in early. I just really love being in a duck blind, but, like I said, what were Dave and I supposed to do?" William continued after taking a reflective sip of his beverage, "So there we were, back at the docks at eleven in the morning. There really wasn't anything open at that time of year on the Outer Banks in those days, so after we'd gone and looked at the ducks in the refuge pond behind the Bodie Island lighthouse, there wasn't much else to do. We ended up at the Salty Dog tavern where Pirate's Cove Yacht Club is now. We figured we'd get a burger and a couple beers. Guess who was playing pinball in the back of the bar when we entered the establishment?"

"What?" I wasn't prepared for the question. "I don't know. Who do you even know on the Banks? One of the old guides," I ventured.

"You're part right. How about guessing 'your guide from the morning?'" William gazed at me balefully as he spun his glass in his hands. He waited for me to comprehend.

"You mean, Marvin? But why was he…oh…oh…oh, criminy! He made up the whole bit about his girlfriend."

William cracked up again. "He got us good, the bastard," William roared. He and the rest of the hunters were all laughing and slapping each other on their backs. Things finally calmed down.

I had to know from a professional standpoint, "But what did he say?" I asked. I'd love to have seen his face when you tapped him on the shoulder," I commiserated.

"Oh, I never said anything to him," William explained. "If I had, I'd have had to punch him…."

I could see the truth in that. We sat there, William and I, nursing our drinks for a few minutes. Finally, William broke the silence.

"You know I wouldn't monkey-wrench you at this time of night. I'll hunt with Marvin tomorrow. I've kind of been looking forward to it," William said under his breath, but he had that evil little grin playing with his lips as he said it.

This time, I cracked up. Partially because of the relief that I didn't have to rearrange all of the parties I'd already arranged (and for that matter, who in the room who had heard the story would even hunt with him now). Mostly, I cracked up because I knew how evil a properly motivated William could be.

So, the next day plays out. At precisely seven that evening, I'm back in the Sea Ranch bar arranging the next day's hunt. When I spy William, I hustle over.

"How'd it go?" I asked hesitantly, afraid to ask, but dying to know.

"Beautifully," William answered. "I'm a changed man," he averred.

"What? No problems?" I probed.

"Absolutely not. In fact, I believe I've had an epiphany," was the curious reply.

"An epipha…what?" This was not the discussion I thought I'd be having.

"I've sat with the Buddha," William gushed while batting his eyes. He feigned nearly fainting. "I am enlightened!" William nearly shouted as he flung his head back and his arms over his head as his eyes rolled into the back of his head and he gazed, sightless, upon the heavens. After a few moments, William gazed apologetically around the room and composed himself. The guys who had been in the bar the night before started to sidle toward us, assuming the conclusion to the story from the night before could be interesting.

William caught my gaze in his. "Buy me a drink and you will be edified," he promised.

What could I do? I bought us both a drink and leaned on the bar. I had decided to let William talk when he was ready. After much posturing, drink sipping and lip smacking due to the skills of the bar's mixologist, William was finally ready to talk.

"This morning started out pretty much the same as did my previous gunning experience with Marvin," William began. My heart started sinking.

"Sparkly red boat lit up by the Q-beam, million-candle-power spotlight." William mocked shielding his eyes, squinting and flailing about blindly. "Some discussion about camping gear…discussion as per route to blind. We went my way," William informed. "Same issue with the decoys, but we agreed he'd do it my way, reluctantly on his part, I'm afraid," he continued. "Thankfully, he'd given up on the dog and left her at home. When he finally skidded Sparkly Red up to the blind and demanded to know where our birds were, I was only too happy to inform him that we had knocked down exactly one drake redhead, which was presently drifting toward the inlet."

"What!" Marvin fairly screamed. 'What about all the buffs?" he demanded.

"We aren't shooting those today!" William reported. "I don't think he remembered me until that moment," William cooed, savoring the recollection of the moment. "Slowly, Marvin's eyes narrowed."

"I remember you. So, you're only shooting drake buffs again."

"You could tell he was figuring how long it would take to run enough drake birds to the blind to limit out. He started to reach for the key to restart the big honkin' motor when I told him — in no uncertain terms — to go get the redhead that was floating away and then to return directly to the boat hide where Sparkly Red was to be parked unless birds were to be retrieved. Period!"

"I further told Marvin that, no, he could not run back to the dock, no, nothing. He was going to spend the day waiting to shoot 'good' ducks with us, and we were not leaving until the sun had set in the west. Period!" William looked about the room, seemingly very proud of himself for standing up to the recalcitrant guide.

"How'd that work out for you?" I had to ask.

"Good. It led me to my visit with the Buddha," was William's reply.

"What?"

"When Marvin got back to the blind with the redhead, he had a trash bag with him," William explained. "Mind you now, this was at about eleven this morning and the sun was up pretty good. So, Marvin goes about cleaning all — every bit — of the trash from out of his blind...and the sun hit the shiny sides of the red and green channel markers that are the floor...." William's voice was rising now and his arms spread and he threw his head back as though he were preaching to the masses. "And then, the very air crackled, and the red and green shine grew and coalesced until an aurora formed around the very blind we were seated in and — yea — it was beautiful!" William let his head fall to his chest and clasped his hands, as if in prayer.

The guys eavesdropping tittered a bit and stood around nervously, not at all sure where this story was going. I was right there with them.

"William," I prodded after enough time had passed.

"And then I saw Buddha," William proselytized in his most fervid voice as he flung his arms out and head back again. "Halleluliah!" he exclaimed for good measure. He stayed in this position for a full minute.

Finally, "Um...William," I interjected. "But, what in the hell are you talking about?"

William snapped down his head and locked his gaze with mine. He started to laugh, "That big fat f...f...f...flower (was the word William settled on) decided that if we were going to spend the day camping, why then he — by God — was going to work on his tan. And, with that, Marvin ripped off his coat and sweater and shirt and...his undershirt!" William was roaring now, as were the bar patrons.

"You should have seen him," William gasped between guffaws, "The blind is in full aurora and there lay Marvin behind the blind with his white pasty skin stretched over that enormously prodigious belly," William choked out. "I have seen the Buddha and he is Marvin!"

A CONVERSATION WITH VERN: REFUGE OF THE MIND

There's something very compelling about the act of immersing yourself as a predator in nature. In many folks' minds, there isn't a better place to do it than in a duck blind. One of duck hunting's bigger draws is that, while in the act of doing so, you get fabulous one-on-one time with your kid(s)…your Dad… your sweetie…your buddies…your business associates. You get the idea.

Photo courtesy Troy Cranford.

The thing is, you can see stuff that is so intense while afield that it can change who you are and how you see yourself and others. That can be pretty heady stuff.

There's an awesome feeling available for a guide when he can share his best-ever or first-ever moments with people. I've had best-ever days with guys nearly eighty years old. I've been there when kids shoot their first-ever ducks. I remember almost hyperventilating when I shot my first-ever tundra swan and, subsequently, have been able to provide that thrill for dozens. I've probably helped better than a hundred guys get their first-ever drake pintails, and being that we harvest an average of twenty-five species per season, I've been involved in all sorts of first-evers with our clients. Taxidermists love me.

Also, what I try to impress on the guides is that our clients only hunt with us for one, or a couple, or a few days of any waterfowl season, but they've been thinking about the trip for the past year. In some cases, I've had guys getting our postcards every season for decades and have been fantasizing about gunning with us for all that time. When they do finally book a trip, it'd be nice if the guide put in his best effort.

I remember one of our first hunts together after my Dad got back from his tour in Vietnam. Even though he was a member of the clergy, Vern's nature wouldn't allow him to hide behind a passive role in the conflict and hide out on base. He really couldn't have if he'd been so inclined because the enemy in the conflict took matters as seriously as did the U.S. forces.

Vern was in-country for the tail end of the Tet offensive and had his entire base overrun on one occasion. That he was quick-witted enough to roll out of his bunk onto the floor and crawl out of his hooch saved his life the first time that night as a chest-high line of bullet holes left in the hooch walls attested. The second instinct that saved his life that night was to not crawl under his hut and hide there, but to instead run for the nearest underground bunker. The several hand grenades that exploded under his hooch as he ran for the bunker only served to hurry him along with more urgency.

Even though it wasn't required, Vern kept returning to the front lines to minister to the young troops, perform last rites and comfort the wounded whenever he could. He felt these functions to be his most important duties during his tour. Numerous times, he would already be driving back from the front in the morning as the mine sweepers finally arrived to clear the roads. When he couldn't get to the front lines via a jeep, he'd have to catch a ride on a chopper. Space on the choppers was extremely limited, so the only way that the pilots could give him the lift was to have him take the space of the machine-gunner. He did this so often that he qualified for an airman's medal at the end of his tour. Of course, the war bosses couldn't actually give him that medal, being he was the preacher, the fifty cal. and all the baggage that goes with that.

I only learned these things over a period of time in Vern's more unguarded moments because he didn't talk much about his time over there. It was his way of trying to shield us kids so that we had more time to grow up. I should've thanked him more for that.

On this particular day's hunt, Vern opened up more than he usually did. I'll never forget the mood. I have no earthly idea if we even shot at any ducks that day. I have to believe that it may have been one of the more important hunts of my life, however.

"Hey, Vic?"

"Yeah, Dad."

"You want to know something funny?"

"Sure."

"This is real important."

There was a pause that went on for too long. Finally, I asked, "Okay, what's real important?"

"This is."

"The word, 'this'?"

"No, the day, the marsh, the birds, the smells...." Vern's voice faded off.

"Yeah, I like that stuff too," I agreed, while scanning the skies for any wayward fowl.

"Hmm," was Vern's response.

One of life's fortunate coincidences is that sometimes unrelated activities, when combined, provide beneficial results. When two people talk in a duck blind, if they situate themselves at each end of the blind and face each other, they can scan all 360 degrees of sky while they converse. Since this is how we arranged ourselves whenever we were gunning in a box blind, I had a good view of Vern's face as we spoke. I could see there was a lot going on in his mind.

"This is what I thought about when things'd get bad over there," Vern offered, kind of under his breath.

This time it was my turn, "Hmm," was my response. I sensed that there was more he wanted to say.

"There was some hairy stuff over there. Really scary...really." He took a while and swallowed a couple times before continuing. You could see that stuff was playing out behind his eyes. When he continued, it startled me a little.

"There were a few times I didn't think I'd make it."

"Oh," I responded, with nothing better to offer. It didn't matter, because Vern was as much unburdening himself as talking to me.

"And that's where the funny part was," he continued. "When I thought I was in a spot I might not get out of, or it was so intense I wasn't so sure if I even wanted to, my mind would kind of shut itself down as I awaited the inevitable. Your body got itself ready to be consumed and, in being so near in your mind, in some ways you do die in small bits."

I didn't understand all of what he was saying, or the implications at the time, but I knew enough that this was not the time to interrupt him. I waited till he was ready to share more…or not. It was up to him. It was probably fifteen minutes before he spoke again.

"I tried to think about your Mom and you kids, but the worse things got, the more my mind would bring me back to remembering times in a duck blind." He shook his head a little. I think he was attempting to shake fear loose from the grip it had on his immortal soul. I don't think he was ever able to shake it loose, entirely.

I have, and have had, many friends and clients who feel this strongly, and find this much peace, in relation to their times afield. Many times, I've been told that the goal in a struggle to stave off death has been the desire to see one more hunt, one more day afield with God and nature painting your day with weather and fowl, intimate conversation, while the wind in your face massages your very being…and there is peace.

And, it is…good.

BLIND THOUGHTS

Vern was one of those wickedly astute kind of guys. He never talked down to me, even as a little kid, and he would take the time to explain what I couldn't understand, but no one was ever allowed sloppy thinking.

As a preacher, Vern's job in his role as a military chaplain involved lots of one-on-one counseling of the young men who make up the vast majority of the armed forces.

As such, a lot of what we talked about was different counseling strategies. Most of what I learned from these discussions was how to look at all sides of an argument, with no particular side of any argument holding more importance than any other side.

This was frustrating for anybody trying to make an actual decision. Vern would convince you of the "pro" of an argument. When you agreed with him on that, he would then examine the "anti" of the argument and, before long, would prove that to you. After that, he would come up with another facet of the argument you'd never thought of and convince you of that as well. He could keep this up till you were about batty.

Finally, in the end you had to make your own decisions, but at least you would have thoroughly examined the subject. Sometime during all of the hours spent gunning and fishing together, my brain must have wired itself along these lines as well. I became, as Vern put it, kind of cursed with perception. I can see why people do what they do and how they got to where they are, but we can't make them opt differently. Free will is a blessing, a freedom, and a curse, but it is your own.

Finally, you understand the unpleasant reality that most choose along the lines of their own best interests, which is rarely anybody else's best interest. It doesn't change anything knowing this, but forewarned is forearmed.

When a Hunt is More than a Hunt

Vern gunned with Jimmy the very first time on December 20, 1966. It was a clear day with just a hint of a south wind, and the temperature topped out at around sixty. They got a late start and hunted from 7:30 until 11 in the morning.

They were gunning blind number eighteen in the Park Service's Bodie Island marsh. They had one flock of Canada geese decoy to them all morning. Jimmy killed one with his sixteen gauge, Winchester, Model Twelve pump gun. Vern hit two geese, hard, but they wouldn't fall.

What they shot that day wasn't really of importance... no, what was important was their recognition of the other as kindred spirits. Vern began gunning with Jimmy in his Kitty Hawk blinds the very next day, and they remained gunning buddies till the end of their days.

A bond formed on that hunt that has affected thousands of outdoorsmen over the decades. What that bond has meant to me is beyond measure.

Photo courtesy Troy Cranford.

Photo courtesy Troy Cranford.

The Power of Guidance

Nonhunters and others who "just do not understand" probably cannot fathom the role that a proficient guide enjoys. For those, let's see if you can answer the following riddle: What's the difference between a duck guide/outfitter and the rest of humanity?

The answer: An attorney will personally answer a call from his guide/outfitter. Also feel free to insert any other high-end occupation. They pay us to sit with them, and they seek our advice.

I personally stood and watched my Dad tell General Patton (the son of the famous one) to *#*# himself, and he didn't get shot in the face or anything. Actually, the General liked it...probably because he knew he deserved it, and I surmise that he hadn't been called out on anything for quite a while. I thought his entire entourage was going to faint, fight or flee, but I'd never been prouder of my Dad.

I don't care who you are — when you're in a guide's care, the guide is in charge and you will answer the phone when he calls...because you want to!

GLOSSARY

Bag: The quarry you actually bring home at the end of a day afield.

Bag limit: The maximum number of any critter you are allowed to harvest on any one day, both total and species. Example: you are allowed six ducks overall, but only three of those can be mallards. Of those three mallards, only one can be a hen.

Bait: Illegal food to attract harvestable critters. For ducks I understand that corn works best, but any whole grain will do. At least that's what the criminals that I know have told me. Being that baiting is illegal, grain that cannot be spotted from an airplane would seem most advantageous. Another entire, interesting book could be written chronicling ne'er do wells' attempts to circumvent baiting laws.

Baiting: The act of putting food into the wilds for diabolical purposes.

Band(s): Aluminum bands that the federal government places on captured ducks' legs to track their movements and life spans. Each band is stamped with an identifying number which is supposed to be reported back to the banding agency. Hunters covet the bands as trophies to be worn on their call lanyards.

Black(s), Black Ducks: A puddle duck that is regarded as the out and out smartest of all the ducks. Usually they travel as singles or pairs. They are famous for circling your rig and deciding whether to land or not…usually not.

Black Bellied Whistling Duck: A very rare tree duck that is mostly only found along rivers of the extreme southern U. S. They are extremely rare anywhere else in North America.

Blind: Anything that somebody hides in to ambush critters from.

Blind Retrieve: Any bird that a dog is supposed to find that he/she didn't actually see fall. A double blind retrieve is when there are two birds involved.

Bling: Federal duck bands in particular but private banding concerns also exist; usually these private bands are found on pen-raised and released birds.

Boat hide: A frame to be brushed you can slide your boat into so that you hunt out of your boat. A drawback is that the boat moves and bobs, especially while you're trying to shoot.

Box Blind: A typical box blind is constructed around a four- by eight-foot sheet of plywood and seats three fairly comfortably; four is doable, but crowded. The walls are also sheets of plywood. The front and back walls are whole, framed, sheets and the side walls are a sheet cut exactly in half. The door will be cut out of one of the side walls. I build my box blinds in five pieces under the house so I have the benefit of electricity: the floor system and the four walls are framed in with two by four studs and then loaded onto an empty boat trailer for transport to the nearest boat ramp to the blind to be constructed.

Brant: A small, somewhat dimwitted goose who has a preference for salt water. Their wing bones are particularly thin and brittle so it sometimes seems that you only need aim near these critters to bring them down. They also have a trait when they land where the birds at the front of the flock stop in the air over your decoys so the birds in the rear of the flock pile up on the birds in front. Knocking down numerous birds per shot is not uncommon. Bad shots love hunting brant.

Brush: The flora that you attach to your blind that makes it disappear and blend in with its' surroundings. Mostly utilized when available are six to ten foot tall pine saplings. A normal sized box blind and attached boat hide eat up almost exactly three hundred saplings. I have nine blinds to build or repair and then to brush every season. As a point of reference, a Toyota pick-up with a camper shell can only fit thirty two to thirty five trees per trip…that's some whacky math.

Bush(ing): Cutting, transporting and affixing flora to your duck blind.

Can(s): Canvas back ducks. In my mind, the canvasback is the king of all the ducks, a diver duck of renowned toughness and verve. Of all the ducks, a male canvasback most deserves the honor of being referred to as a bull!

Canvasback: A diver duck. Easily in any top three water fowl in regards to the taste and texture of its breast meat. My personal top three tastiest water fowl would be Cans, pintail and teal, with woodies in a near tie with the teal.

Chessie: A Chesapeake Bay retriever; the toughest of all the retriever dogs; also the nuttiest and most loyal. It is literally almost impossible to hunt one of these dogs hard enough.

Coot: A small, jet black, water fowl with a white bill and the mannerisms of a chicken hen. They appear to be kind of goofy and are probably more closely related to a rail bird than a duck. They travel in large flocks and eat the same stuff that ducks eat. Their breast meat and legs are perfect for inclusion in a gumbo. Just remember to soak the meat in butter milk before cooking and adding to your gumbo.

Cracked Corn: The bait of choice for the truly chronic law offender. "Cracked" means that the outer skin of the corn kernel is broken. Because of this the kernel absorbs the color of the water that it is in and therefore becomes invisible after it's had time to soak. Hence, you need to bait at dusk. At least that's what I've been told.

Decoys: Anything that appears to be a live bird that will lure real birds into shotgun range. The best and most rudimentary decoy that I ever used was hand shaped blobs of eelgrass that we tossed onto the edge of an open air hole on the frozen-over sound. They looked exactly like sleeping black ducks and worked fabulously.

Divers: The group of water fowl that favor large, open water. They dive freely while feeding. Their legs are set farther back on their bodies. From shoulder to tail a diver's legs are a third closer to the tale. As comparison a puddle duck's legs are set in the middle between shoulder and tail so that they balance better while standing.

Drake: A male duck of any species.

Duck calls: Any of a myriad of devices utilized to mimic the sounds that various ducks make. The mallard call is the most well known with its nyack, nyack, nyack highball call. FYI: Of the thirty-two water fowl available for harvest in North America, only the mallard makes this call. Most of the fowl that I prefer to hunt make whistling or purring calls. Contrary to most gunners, I rarely grab my mallard "highball" call.

Duck Lice: Yes, ducks can have lice. And, yes they will scamper up your arm on occasion while you're plucking your ducks. If it makes it all the way to the hair on your head you need a faithful spouse to hunt it down and kill it for you. Always roll your sleeves way up when you pluck ducks. Just so you can rest easier, I only had a duck louse make it to my hairline twice in fifty years of gunning.

Duck Season: You are only allowed to harvest ducks while they are on their wintering grounds, which is during early to dead-middle winter. In the mid-Atlantic states (where we are), we have a series of seasons with the emphasis on December till the end of January.

European Widgeon: A very rare puddle duck which is native to the European continent. A handful (for whatever reason) migrate across the top of the polar ice caps and winter within the confines of the Atlantic flyway. I had one whack at a "Euro" that I know of in fifty years of water fowling. (That also includes all of the clients who gunned with me personally during all of those decades.)

Gaddies: Gadwall, a puddle duck. Probably the most vexing of all ducks due to their tendency to set their wings and head directly into the heart of your decoy spread, only to fall off at the last second and sit just on the far outer edge of your shotgun's lethal range.

Gadwall: A puddle duck. Their voice is an odd quack that sounds kind of similar to a wet fart. I've got a call that actually does an enticing wet fart imitation. That it works on occasion keeps it on my call lanyard.

Goldeneyes: A diving duck hardy enough to often be lumped in with the sea ducks. They are shot only on the edges of large, cold bodies of water.

Gunwale: Pronounced gunnel. The edge of the boat that you lean on and look over as you gaze at the water. This is a very dynamic area as anything and everybody coming into or out of a boat has to cross over/through the gunwale. If you fall out of a boat the gunwale was involved.

Harlequin duck: A diving duck from the "great White North." If you don't see ice, you're probably not going to see a harlequin. The males are a gorgeous blue color over-all, with splotches of burnt sienna and patterns of white. I heard of only one in North Carolina since I began gunning here in 1963.

Layout Boat: A low sided boat painted to match the water or brushed to look like a small island. You lay down in it to hide and sit up to shoot. They are hideous torture devices to gun out of properly. They are cold and damp and, for some reason, cause your butt to itch like fire once you've lain in one for any amount of time. I know they can be very effective in the right circumstances, but I am not a big fan.

Limit: The most ducks you are legally allowed to harvest in a day.

Mallards: The most sought after puddle duck. They're big, consistently tasty and when they're in a mood to, can pitch into your decoys heroically. You can be a real hero if you're patient and skilled enough to pick off only the green-headed drakes while hunting.

Mergansers: Water fowling's horns of a dilemma. They taste lousy but they fly well. If you're not going to eat them, then you shouldn't shoot them. The only accepted exception is the occasional harvesting for the benefit and training of your retriever dog.

Nor'easter: A low pressure weather system that forms in the ocean off of Florida and rides the coast up through New England. A brutal weather phenomenon by definition, it creates strong, north winds, cold temperatures and rain/sleet/snow.

Nutria: A large, ugly, Russian marsh rat with a terrible attitude. They're mean! I've had to shoot a few of these psychotic thugs who had ambushed my dog a couple different times. Thirty-five to forty-pound beasts are not uncommon. Nutrias' species-wide trait of feeding on marsh plant roots results in wide-spread marsh destruction.

Picking out drakes: Given a choice, don't shoot the hens. My clients and I once ran off a streak of twenty-seven straight pintail (over a period of a few weeks) without harvesting a hen. The implication of such a streak is that it means the entire twenty-seven bird run had absolutely zero effect on the pintail's overall breeding success the next year. Those drakes that survive to breed happily take up the slack.

Picking Up: Gathering up all of your decoys at the end of your hunt.

Pintail: The other most sought after fowl besides the canvasback. A puddle duck, and elegantly mannered fowl. They fly pretty, decoy perfectly and are an epicurean delight. Their two central tail feathers form a long (ten- to twelve-inch), slender spike. This spike, or pin, or sprig, when combined with a pintails' bold color patterns, makes a male pintail the most identifiable of all the ducks. During the 2011/2012 gunning season our (OBW) guide service harvested 196 Pintail. I would predict that 178 of those were drakes.

Pitch: The final approach of a landing water fowl. When any water fowl flies it is always flapping its wings. The only time ducks coast while flying is during landing. That final coast is called pitching into the decoys/rig. Being able to watch ducks pitch into my decoys is what brings me back duck hunting day after day, year after year and decade after decade.

Puddlers: The grouping of duck species that tip up to feed as opposed to diving. This means that a puddler can only feed in water that is less than half their combined body and neck length in depth.

Redheads: A diver duck named for its obvious coloring. Redhead drakes are black fore and aft, white in the middle, and have a bright, burnt sienna-colored, candy apple-looking head. They are probably the second most sought after diver duck after the canvasback.

Rig: The entirety and shape of all your decoys that you put out to hunt over at any given time. By the shape of your rig, I mean how the clusters of decoys (seen as patterns from a point above and looking down on) have been arranged by the decoy setter.

Rigging: The act of setting out and arranging your decoys.

Ruddies: A diver duck. They are a very small duck, but, proportionately, have large succulent slabs of breast meat. During the period when market hunting was allowed — up till, I believe, 1918 — the diminutive ruddies' cost per pair was second only to pairs of canvasbacks. Accordingly ,ruddies were referred to as dollar ducks.

Scaup: A diver duck. Actually there are two species of scaup; greater and lesser. They are also known as blackheads or bluebills.

Set wings: When fowl quit flapping their wings and coast, pre-landing.

Shore blind: A duck blind built on land or the edge of a shoreline.

Sprig: The two long, central, tail feathers that give the pintail it's name.

Sou'wester: A strong wind from the southwest, which is usually associated with warm temperatures, high water, and torrential rain. Usually the leading edge of an eventual nor'easter.

Teal: The smallest and second tastiest puddle duck. The three species of teal are green wing, blue wing, and cinnamon. The cinnamon are extremely rare along the U.S. Atlantic coast. Teal are most excellent targets.

Tip/Tipping: A puddle duck in the act of feeding or a guide's measure of worth at the end of a day.

Tertials: A feather group along the back of a bird's wing. When a bird coasts to land, the rapid descent creates a vacuum, and then lift, to this set of feathers so extreme that they can chatter or hum due to the vibration created by the rapid descent. I've had a squadron of ringnecks tumble over a tree canopy into a deeply wooded pond I was hunting with such abandon that their vibrating tertials sounded like crackling electricity powerful enough to awaken Frankenstein.

Widgeon: A puddle duck. One of my all-time favorite ducks. We shoot lots from my marsh. They often fly in flocks of six to twenty-six. They decoy readily, fall easy, and taste great.

Wings set: The act of fixing the wings and starting to coast prior to landing.